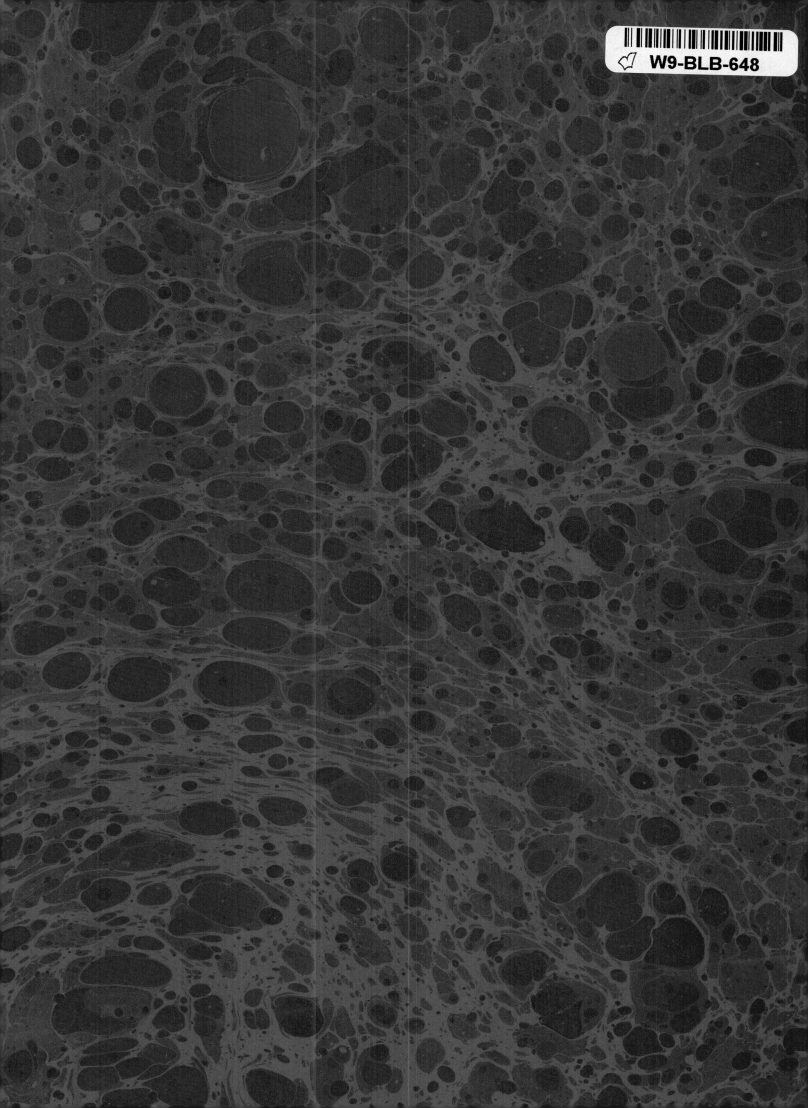

The Enchanted World

WIZARDS AND WITCHES

The Enchanted World

WIZARDS AND WITCHES

by Brendan Lehane
and the Editors of Time-Life Books

The Content

Time-Life Books · Alexandria, Virginia

Chapter One

O

Singers at the World's Dawn

On a day long ago when the world was young, a horse-drawn sleigh swept along the track that cut across a heath in Finland, curling around shining lakes and winding toward dark pine forests where wolves sang.

At the reins of the sleigh was an aged man, heavy-browed and white-bearded. He was Vainamöinen, called the Steadfast, and he was a wizard.

From time to time the farsighted old eyes glanced toward the distant forests that marched along the northern rim of the heath. In the expanse before him, only one thing moved, a tiny speck in the pale, snow-whitened light. Hours passed. The speck grew and took shape as a sleigh, drawn like the wind by a horse whose hoofs struck glittering sparks in the track.

The wizard reined in his horse. But the strange sleigh hurtled on, unerring as an arrow. With a screech, it crashed into his own, locking the sleigh shafts together. Trapped in the tangled harnesses, the horses whinnied and stamped, steam rising from their flanks as the men brought them under control. There followed a brief silence. Vainamöinen regarded the driver of the other sleigh impassively and asked his clan name. The reply was abuse and challenge. The black-bearded youth was Joukahainen, and he had traveled across the Northern wastes from Lapland. He had heard tales of the old wizard's power, how he sang things into being, how he spoke with eagles and summoned water spirits, how his songs made the bleak heath bloom. In his arrogance, Joukahainen had come to enchant the enchanter, to sing him down into the snow forever, and to take his place as sage of the North.

The old man listened and then spoke. "Tell me what you know," he said.

Joukahainen began to chant into the wind, composing a song to show that he possessed a wizard's understanding of the workings of the world. But all that he sang was surfaces, nothing deeper than a child knows. He said that flame was near a fireplace and smoke holes near ceilings, that people plowed with mares in the south and reindeer in the north. He sang of commonplaces: the habits of fish, the methods of farmers and the shapes of the land.

"Speak of more profound matters," said Vainamöinen.

The boy's voice grew louder. He sang of origins. He said that he himself had

At the end of his adventures, the mighty wizard Vainamöinen set sail in a copper boat for a land between the earth and the heavens, far from his Finnish home.

plowed the sea, propped up the sky, guided the moon, flung the stars into the heavens and shaped them into constellations.

"You lie," said Vainamöinen calmly.

Stung, Joukahainen challenged Vainamöinen to a duel of swords. The old man refused. Joukahainen replied with a threat: "If you will not measure swords with me, old one, I will sing you into a swine, into a rooting, grumbling, ground-watching, sty-dwelling pig."

At last Vainamöinen grew angry. He threw back his head and began to sing. Bright, keening melodies fell from the air, and the earth began to move. Mountains trembled, lakes spilled over their shores, great stones split apart.

That was only the beginning. Still singing, the enchanter turned to Joukahainen, and as he sang, bushes sprouted from the sleigh's shaft bow, and the beautiful sleigh itself dwindled into a pile of logs sliding into a lake. The boy's beaded horsewhip disappeared, and in its place stood a frail shore reed; the horse froze into a rock, crouching beside a waterfall. Joukahainen's golden sword exploded as a flash of lightning, and his arrows rose into the sky, sprouting wings. His garments flew off one by one, landing in pools of water or sailing away into the clouds like kites. Joukahainen, cold and naked, began to sink into the boggy earth.

Vainamöinen sang inexorably on, and Joukahainen's feet, heavy as stone, dragged him steadily down. At last the cold earth closed around his shoulders. Joukahainen felt a tiny, icy current tug at his feet and a great fear at his heart, and he began to plead.

"Eternal sage," Joukahainen cried, "reverse the charm and spare my life. Let me pay ransom."

The singing and sinking ceased. "And what will you give me?" the old man asked.

Joukahainen offered splendid crossbows, but Vainamöinen had no need of those. The boy offered a pair of swift boats and a pair of stallions, but the old man had those in plenty. Joukahainen offered silver, but Vainamöinen had silver enough. The Laplander offered the fields that were his birthright, but the old man cared nothing for them. He began to sing again, and Joukahainen slowly sank.

As the shifting ground began to close around his mouth, the boy made a last plea. He offered the enchanter his own young sister, Aino.

And Vainamöinen paused. That was a good thing he did not own, and a fine price for the insult—a glowing girl to comfort his old age. He took the offer. He sat and, with a smile, sang again, once, twice and thrice. His song raised Joukahainen from the bog, drew his clothes from the clouds and water, his sleigh from the lake and his horse from the rock. Joukahainen had his life again, having paid for it with that of his sister.

When the world was in its infancy, truculent youths who aspired to wizardry were well advised to tread softly near their mighty elders. None could measure the power of an ancient wizard's words, as the hapless Joukahainen discovered.

And Vainamöinen was not unique in that age, for other enchanters' names echo across the sundering centuries. With Vainamöinen in Finland were Ilmarinen the Smith, who made a mill that eternally ground out salt, grain and gold; Lemminkäinen, who could sing sand into pearls; and, in the Northern reaches, Louhi the Sorceress, who, storytellers said, once stole the sun and moon and hid them in a mountain. Across the Russian steppes strode the warlike Volga Vseslavich, who could take many forms. In Ireland were Cathbad, who knew the meaning of every hour, and the bard Cairpré, who toppled a tyrant with a quatrain of verse. On the Isle of Man in the Irish Sea dwelt Manannan Mac Lir, whose protective spells could raise a mist to shield his realm or change a single foot soldier into a company of a hundred.

Britain was called the Island of the Mighty, and with reason. In Wales lived Taliesin, son of the sorceress Ceridwen. Math the Ancient, who heard in the wind each word spoken on the island, was Welsh, too, as was Math's nephew Gwyd-

ion, a maker of illusions. And toward that era's end came the greatest of enchanters and the crown of wizardry, Merlin.

Not all of them were good. They lived in a fierce age, and some — like the malevolent Louhi — devoted their powers to the service of darkness. Others — Joukahainen and Gwydion when young — were careless with the weapons they wielded. But the best had greatness of heart to match their magic, and they served as guides and guardians to the lesser folk around them. These were old Vainamöinen, wise Math, sunny-natured Manannan, and Merlin.

The wizards of this time often worked in

Ilmarinen the Smith, a young companion of Vainamöinen and a wizard in his own right, loved the daughter of Louhi, Sorceress of the North. The maiden loved him, too, but Louhi made the wooing a rough one: She charged the young man to defy death three times to win his bride. His first trial was to plow a field full of adders. Shod in iron and guiding a golden plow, Ilmarinen furrowed the adder-ridden ground, singing the serpents out of his path. Then he entered the lands of the dead, seeking a bear and a wolf there; with magic bridles, he took the beasts to Louhi. Lastly, from that same bleak region, the smith obtained a malevolent fish, as the sorceress demanded, capturing it with an eagle he forged and charmed to life. Thus Ilmarinen bested Louhi and had her daughter for his bride.

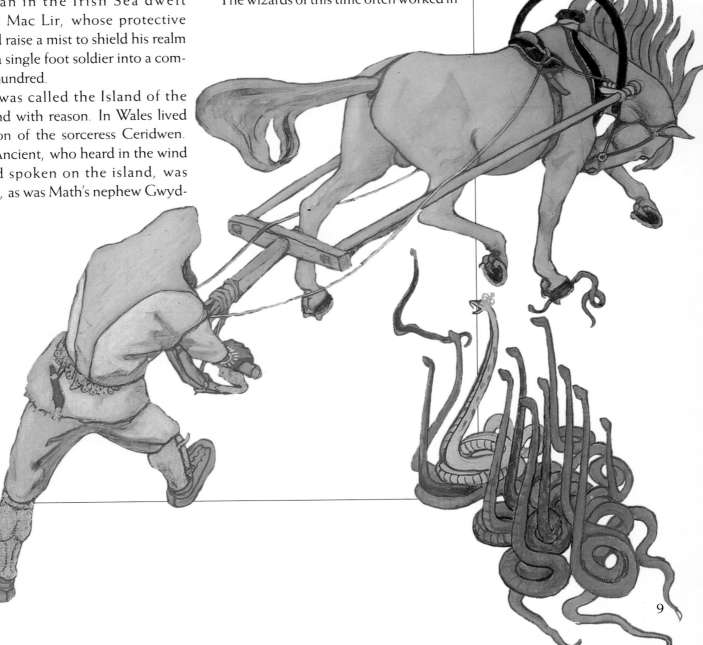

silence off the stage, king-makers and -breakers, so their deeds have come down in fragments of song and tattered scraps of history. To serve their ends, it was said, they harnessed winds and waters when they wished, moved the planets from their pathways, conjured vast concourses of people where none had been before, and changed their own and other people's shapes. They cured or inflicted disease or deformity. They saw into the future.

In later days, when the first enchanters' deeds had become the stuff of legend, some men and women continued to practice the magic arts. But these people lived in a world that had aged and lost its innocence. As the centuries passed, scholars — primarily clerics in the new and growing church — had examined the world around them, naming and ordering its various elements, shapes and patterns. To reach the old, primal magic, wizards had to tamper with the newly perceived order of nature, and this activity came to be viewed as an arrogant and evil pursuit.

The great ones among these later people — Faust, for instance — sometimes were given the titles held by their distinguished predecessors: They, too, were called wizards or enchanters. The former word is grandly all-embracing; "wizard" means at its root "one who is wise," while "enchanter" refers to a true wizard's power with words and incantations. But more often, the powerful among these later magic-workers were called sorcerers or magicians, titles that imply only the ability to see into the future. The humblest were called witches, or "people set apart."

In most cases, those who were adept at

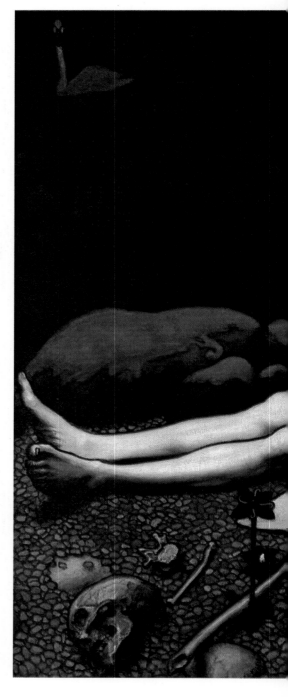

enchantment lacked the natural insight and inborn generosity of the first wizards. Instead, they were introverted seekers after lost or hidden powers, scholars who

Life songs in the lands of the dead

When Finnish poets sang of Vaina-möinen and Ilmarinen, they sang of Lemminkäinen, too. Like Ilmarinen, he sought to win a daughter of the sorceress Louhi, and like Ilmarinen, he dared the lands of the dead, bent on tasks Louhi had set as a bride price. But one of Louhi's people was lurking there and, when Lemmin-käinen came, slew him.

In Finland, Lemminkäinen's mother, a sorceress herself, knew at once of her son's danger, but none of her arts could tell her what the danger was or where the young man had gone. So she set out to find him, heading north across the snow fields, traveling on foot and alone. She was a mistress of disguise, and if Louhi's people had been on watch for her, they would have seen no more than a rabbit on a riverbank or a gray wolf loping among the grasses of the fens.

At length, the mother found the path her son had taken. (The poets say that the sun told her the way, but that might be only the words they chose to express her skill with the lore of track and tree and stars' signs.) She continued far to the north, crossing the border wastes, where the snowy meadows gave way to bone-littered scrub and shadow, and the winds never ceased their sobbing.

At last she came to the black water the poets called Death's River, and from its bed she raked the piteous remnants of the body of her son. Working on the riverbank, she sang spells that made his body whole, bolting the bones together and weaving the flesh. But he was cold. Lemminkäinen's mother sang again, calling fiercely on powers that might animate him. When she finally fell silent, his heart began to beat beneath her hand. Thus the mother gave life to the son again and, having done this, took him back to Finland and safety. But he never won the daughter of the sorceress.

used arcane systems and complex, secret sciences to reach into the mysteries they knew existed just out of sight and almost out of reach. They were explorers breach-ing forbidden seas, and some paid dearly for the treasures they acquired.

Their dark ventures, though, were far in the unimagined future when Vainamöinen and the first enchanters lived. The earth was very new then, and things of the natural world were changeable as opals, or so the chroniclers say.

It was an era when a knight traveling through the rolling fields and pastures and forest-cloaked hills of Wales could come upon a river that had a flock of white sheep grazing on one side and a flock of black sheep grazing on the other; from time to time, a sheep from one flock waded through the water toward the opposite bank, and as it did so, its color changed. The traveler might see mist swathing the turrets of a castle that moments before had gleamed in the sunlight; if he ventured through the gate and into the hall he might find it deserted, save for a golden gaming board on which silver men played a game like chess among themselves, making their moves without the aid of human hands.

A wanderer might glimpse a horse cantering over the surface of the sea as if it were solid turf, or see a man turn into an eagle and soar into the clouds. All of those occurrences and many more were reported and ascribed to the workings of magic.

In a world so shifting and uncertain, it is not surprising that great store was set on all that was not clearly one thing or another. At the in-between places — rivers and borders — and at all edges, verges, brinks, rims, fringes and dividers, anything might happen, and chaos could be loosed upon the world.

It made no difference whether these were borders of space or of time. Caves, the thresholds between open air and the solidity of earth, were often entrances to the world of spirits. Wells linked the visible world with subterranean realms and had an innate enchantment that might give awareness of the future or restore the dead to life. In the space dividing foam and water or bark and tree, devils could be confined by those who knew how.

Certain objects held magic by virtue of this same borderline nature. It was no accident that mistletoe could heal diseases and bring good luck (or sometimes bad) to those who held it. Mistletoe belongs to the edge of the family of plants. It grows not from the ground but in the air, thrusting its roots deep into the bark of hawthorn, oak or rowan trees.

Dew likewise is poised at the limits of definition. Though water, it comes not from sea, river or spring but from the air. It does not flow with gravity but rests lightly on leaf or grass blade. And it comes and goes at yet another borderline, the division between night and day. There were those who thought that dew mysteriously digested sunlight and made it into gold.

Dawn and dusk were magical times, for they divided the fundamental elements of existence: night from day, darkness from light, the period when evil was abroad from the time when it was banished to its secret sanctuaries.

So also the times between the seasons. Among the Celtic peoples of Ireland, Britain and France, winter began at Samhain, the first of November, later called All Hallows Day. On the prior evening, the rules of reality were suspended, the air was more dangerously charged with magical power than at any other time, and the spirits of other worlds were free to roam. The eve of Beltane, or May Day, which marked the beginning of summer, was another crack through which primeval magic entered.

Unseen powers were at play in those days, in those times and places. Only a few men and women understood these powers and—through that understanding—controlled them. The early wizards possessed great knowledge, which sprang from the very nature of their being. Through their brains and veins and sinews, the cordial of magic flowed like blood. In greater or lesser degree, they contained in their bodies the very elements that made the world so restless. The greatest, though men or women in form, encapsulated something of the nature of animals, plants, winds, thunder, lightning, moon and stars—all the things in heaven and earth, one could almost say. They were both human and superhuman.

It is no wonder that strange tales about their births arose. Vainamöinen, his people said, was fathered by the winds and waves on the Air Virgin of Finland as she floated on the primeval sea; he rested thirty years in his mother's womb before emerging to become the much-sung wizard of his country. Merlin's maiden mother had never known a human man; his father was an incubus, a seeming man who visited the young woman at night, no more than a transient dream. Of Taliesin, many of whose later deeds are shrouded in the mists of time and cryptic poetry, they told a strange birth-tale indeed.

A sorceress named Ceridwen, the story

The island enchantress

Far to the south of the lands of the first enchanters, on a forest-shrouded island in the Adriatic Sea, lived the sorceress Circe. Her companions were tame bears and wolves and swine that had once been sailors. Ever malignant, she had lured them ashore by the magic of her singing and transformed them with spells.

Sailors were not her only victims. Another was a charming nymph named Scylla, whose habit it was to bathe at the edge of the island. She attracted the sorceress's attention because of her shepherd lover, whom Circe found desirable.

Circe, therefore, walked alone one night among tall pines to the place where Scylla bathed in the mornings. She poised herself on a rock and raised high a crystal bowl she bore. Into the sea she poured a liquid, green as emerald. She watched a moment while the spell-strengthened bubbles danced away and dissolved. Then, well satisfied, she disappeared.

At dawn, the sweet-voiced nymph came singing to the shore. She stepped into the water, admiring the pearly tones it gave her ankles. The colors deepened to green as Scylla stepped farther in, and the tide pulled at her. Then, to her horror, she saw in the swirling water a green and writhing mass, which crept slowly up her thighs and drew her down.

Under the waves, Scylla changed. When her head reappeared, it was hideous, split and fanged and slavering. The voice that came from it was a bestial howl. Thus transformed, Scylla became a terror to sailors of that sea. As for Circe, she lived long on her pine-covered island; although whether she enjoyed the favors of Scylla's shepherd no one knows, for the tale does not tell what became of him.

13

begins, lived on a mountain lake in Penllyn in Wales. Some chroniclers claim the palace was under the waters of the lake, but this is unlikely, and most sources place it on an island. In any event, Ceridwen bore a son named Morfran, so repellently ugly that he was nicknamed Afagddu, or "Utter Darkness." Ceridwen was determined that he have wisdom to compensate for his appearance — a body as hairy as a stag's and a demeanor so horrid people thought him a demon — and to this end she studied deeply in the magical arts.

Finally she discovered a means of giving Morfran all the knowledge of the world, as well as the gift of prophecy. She had only to pick certain herbs at the times when they were most potent and boil them in a caldron for a year and a day. At the end of that period, three drops of the brew would spring from the caldron, fall on the boy and make him an enchanter.

Ceridwen gathered her herbs and engaged an old blind man to tend the caldron for the brewing. The old man's name is not important to the story. He had a boy with him who served as his eyes, and that boy's name is famous now. It was Gwion Bach.

For a year and a day, in the depths of Ceridwen's castle, the man and the boy stirred the magic brew and kept the caldron's fire blazing. The sorceress added herbs at the prescribed times, and as the year drew to a close, she stationed her son beside the caldron. Then she rested.

This was a mistake, for at the moment when the brew's bubbling indicated that the magic potion had reached its final stages, the silent churl Gwion Bach, the blind man's guide, pushed Morfran aside so that when the three magic drops sprang from the caldron they fell on him instead of on Ceridwen's son. With a wailing shriek the caldron cracked, the liquid in it streaming into the fire below. Ceridwen awoke.

Chaos followed. Gwion Bach now was possessed of a wizard's intuition, which told him that the thwarted enchantress would kill him if she could. He turned and began to run, with Ceridwen at his heels. Through the echoing corridors of the palace ran Gwion Bach, with the sorceress ever close behind him. When he found a way out, he suddenly changed into a hare for fleetness and headed across the grass. He glanced back, and where Ceridwen might have been, he saw instead a greyhound with its teeth bared, running like the wind, stretched out lean and low to the ground. Gwion reached the island's shore and at once dived into the lake, using his newly won powers to change into the shape of a fish. He sped away among the swaying water reeds, but at his tail was an otter, lithe, brown and deceptively

"I am a musician, an artificer like the wren," sang the Welsh wizard Taliesin, and it was true: His songs were about creation and transformation, and they made those magical things occur.

A brew of wisdom concocted by the sorceress Ceridwen for her son instead touched the boy Gwion Bach and made him a wizard. In animal forms, she pursued the boy; as an animal she ate him; as a woman she bore him again. Thus, by magic, he became the enchanter Taliesin.

sweet-faced. The dainty otter paw grazed his tail, and Gwion shot to the surface.

He broke water, changing into the form of a swift, fleetest of birds. But as he flew off, he saw far above him, mounting in easy spirals, a great, long-winged hawk. In an instant it stooped, rocketing toward him, talons at the ready.

Gwion dropped toward the earth again, and as he dropped he shrank and shifted his shape to that of a grain of wheat. He landed on a winnowing floor, surrounded by thousands of other grains exactly like himself. For a moment all was still. But a black hen appeared, picking her way fussily through the littered floor, cocking her head sideways in her hennish way so that the round red eye stared straight down into the wheat. She hunted and pecked and cackled under her breath. She pecked at a grain and discarded it. Finally she came to the grain that was Gwion Bach. The sharp little beak descended and the hen snatched the grain and swallowed.

The black hen ruffled out her feathers and swelled until she once again took the form of Ceridwen. But now the sorceress carried within her the seed of an enchanter, and nine months later she was delivered of an exquisite son. She wanted to rid herself of him, but she had not the heart to murder the beautiful child. Instead, she tucked him into a coracle—a tiny, hide-covered basket—and ordered him cast into the waters.

Some say the sorceress had the child put into the sea, some say a lake, some a river. In any case, the coracle did not sink but drifted until it reached a weir—a dammed-up tidal pond—at the edge of the sea near Castell Deganwy in the north of Wales. The weir was famous in that kingdom, for every year at the Eve of Samhain it cast up rich salmon. In that particular year, a lord's son, Elphin, came to the weir in search of the fish. What he found instead was the coracle. He drew back the wrappings and saw the shining forehead of a child.

Elphin cried, "Behold the radiant brow." That phrase in Welsh was *Tal iesin*, and to Elphin's astonishment the infant replied, "Taliesin he is!"

As it happens, the most that is known of Taliesin's life concerns his childhood and youth. The young Lord Elphin was a spendthrift and a rather silly man, but he seems to have had a good heart. He placed the coracle in the saddlebag of one of his horses and took the infant home to his wife, who cared for the boy, the scribe says, "lovingly and dearly."

Even in infancy, Taliesin was a singer, and he grew into that most beloved of Celts, a bard whose poetry had magical powers. He became a kindly supporter of his foster father, bringing him prosperity and saving him from trouble when need be. When Elphin was wrongfully imprisoned for boasting at the court of his king, Taliesin charmed his fetters off. Then, before the assembled court, the young man sang of his miraculous origins and prophesied, in poignant verses, the coming invasions of Britain by the Saxons.

The mark of all the great enchanters was their profound knowledge of words and of that best ordering of words, poetry. Now-

adays, when words float cheap as thistledown, people only faintly recall the worth and power they once possessed. Words gave order and shape to reality: To know the name of a thing was to perceive its essence and therefore to master it. To name a thing not present was to summon it into being, so that the thing itself existed in the words for it. "I was many things before I was released," sang Taliesin once. "I was a word in letters." A name could be moved and manipulated and placed in new arrangements, and all of these activities would affect the object named. It is no wonder that people at that time were very reluctant to reveal the true names of their gods, their countries and themselves.

The outward sign of the inner powers of a wizard was his knowledge of words and names and the songs he made from them. That is why Joukahainen's challenge to Vainamöinen began with a recitation of all the things he knew about the world, and why Celtic wizards such as Taliesin prefaced their spells with transformation songs—verses that claimed they had taken the shape of everything in creation, from raindrops and starlight to bubbles in beer, and thereby had gained infinite understanding. Words were the bricks of all charms and incantations, all spells, riddles and conjurations. Words, it was said, could blind, maim and pulverize. They could cause kings to lose their thrones, as an Irish tale attests:

There was a time, this tale begins, when Ireland was ruled by a grasping, morose bully of a sovereign by the name of Bress. He taxed his unhappy subjects mercilessly and laid additional levies on their homes and possessions, down to the boards the women used for kneading dough. He was cunning in his avarice, too. He proposed to his people that the milk of every hairless brown cow in Ireland should be his. Since a bald cow is a rare cow, the people readily agreed. Bress immediately gathered all the brown cows of the country and passed them between two fires to singe off their hair. He was, as the Irish liked to say, father and grandfather to a fox. But he was arrogant and therefore careless.

One day a bard and a wizard named Cairpré came to Bress's palace. Poets being held in high regard, it was both customary and prudent to invite such a visitor to stay as long as he liked and to take his meals at the high table in the hall, along with the King and courtiers.

Bress was far too mean. He had the poet lodged in a bare, cold attic, where no more than a trencher of dry bread was carried to him by an ugly serving girl. Cairpré knew the proper order of things, the patterns of behavior that kept the small world safe from the dark. He knew what made a worthy king and what was due a wizard. Every feeling was offended. He announced that he was leaving, and when he did so, he was summoned, as he expected, before the King to give the usual poem of thanks to his host. Bress talked to his counselors throughout the recitation and therefore did not notice that Cairpré's poem was no lickspittle tribute. Instead, the poet made a little rhyme that wished Bress the kind of treatment he doled out to his guests.

As soon as the poem was done, the King

felt a warm tingling in his cheeks. His companions were horrified to see large red blotches break out over his face. None of Bress's doctors, herbalists or sorcerers could disperse the unsightly rash, and nothing would persuade Cairpré to withdraw his words. Since the law said that Irish monarchs must be without physical blemish, Bress was forced to abdicate—a great relief to his subjects—and all because of a few verses composed extemporaneously by a wizard.

Among enchanters, Taliesin was most famed for his skill with words. Unfortunately, no complete accounts of the songs and deeds of his prime survive. Looking into the past to find him—and many of his fellows, for that matter—is like gazing into the wrong end of a telescope: The image is tiny, and everything important seems to be happening just outside the viewer's field of vision. Taliesin is reported to have appeared at one king's court and then at another's; scattered songs are still remembered. But details are few.

One of Taliesin's songs says that he was present at Cad Goddeu, and fragmented as the story is, it is of interest for the wonders he reports and for the wizard who caused them. Cad Goddeu was a battle, called one of the three futile battles of Britain because the slaughter was brought about for so petty a cause—a white roebuck and a greyhound pup, according to some sources; a deer, dog and lapwing, according to others. The animals—the first of their kind on earth—were taken from Arawn, King of Annwfn, that is to say, from the underworld. The thieves were the sorcerer Gwydion and his brother, and they fought Arawn, successfully, it is said, to keep the prizes.

Taliesin himself does not report the outcome of the battle, but he does describe the initial charge. On the field, Gwydion raised his staff of enchantment, says the bard, and called upon his powers. From the forests around, at his command, strode an army of sentient trees—swift and mighty oaks, ferocious elms, hawthorn, willow, rowan and, tearing to the fore, the stalwart fir trees. The battle got its name because of Gwydion's spells: Cad Goddeu means "the battle of the trees."

Cad Goddeu, in its incomplete way, fits perfectly into the picture of the early enchanters and their deeds. With their magic, they acted upon or through or with things of the natural world—winds and waters, stars and planets, birds, beasts, flowers and trees. Nature was closer to humankind then. There were no teeming cities. The towered castles of warring kings and the fragile huts of peasants stood alike in clearings that seemed small and vulnerable amid the wilderness of the young earth. At night, when magic was most often abroad, the people's feeble rushlights made hardly a glimmer in the darkness that surrounded them. Above them in ordered patterns wheeled the silent, star-fretted heavens, so lucid and close that the moon herself seemed to rest upon the tangled branches of the trees.

All around the little clearings loomed great trees: the oak, said to wail when it was cut; the hawthorn, home to fairies; the ash, which Northerners said held up the sky. Some of these trees had beneficial powers, and some were trees to fear. There

(continued on page 25)

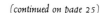

20

Wizard of Kiev

The singers of Russia tell this tale: When the glittering camps of the Golden Horde—the Tartar heirs of Genghis Khan—were spread throughout the frosty Caucasus, the Tartar leaders turned greedy eyes north toward Russia and found themselves matched against the enchanter Volga Vseslavich. Strange tales gathered about his name. His mother was a princess of Kiev, it was said, but his father was a serpent; from the mother came his courage and from the father his skill and guile. At night, he assumed the shape of a lion and hunted forest animals; when he fished for sturgeon, he took the form of a pike. But by day, he was a warrior and a leader of warriors: In his fifteenth year,

he had an army of 7,000, and with it he challenged the Tartars.

It happened this way: Word came to Kiev that in the Caucasus the Golden Horde was arming for invasion. The warrior wizard gathered his officers for counsel, but none would venture a mission across the Russian steppes to spy on the enemy's mountain stronghold. It is said that Volga Vseslavich laughed at the cowardice and in the next moment he vanished from view. In his place stood a ram, which turned at once and sped away. The last the Russians saw of the beast was the flash of its gilded horns at the edge of the distant plain. For long days and nights, through winds and rains, the ram traveled toward the territory of the Khan. At last it halted on a mountain crag and watched a windy plain below, where sentries marched the ramparts of the Khan's fortress. No adversary had breached that stronghold. One hour later, a scarlet-crested

bird lighted at the window of a chamber high in the fortress. It cocked its head to catch the words of the man and woman within.

The bird heard the Khan tell his wife how he would divide the rich Russian lands among his sons. The woman cried, "I dreamed two birds battled: A small Northern bird slew a raven from the South. That small bird was the enchanter Volga; do not raise your arm against him." But the Tartar cursed her dreaming. The listener at the window took wing.

That night a destroyer struck at the fortress: A ferret darted about the armory, tearing bowstrings and snapping arrows with its teeth. By the time the guards heard it, the ferret was gone, and from the stables rose the screams of dying horses. Soldiers there drew swords against

an invisible enemy. Someone saw the shadow of a wolf on the wall; then, someone heard the beating wings of a falcon flying toward Russia. Left weaponless and unmounted, the Tartars were crippled.

But the Russian enchanter wanted more vengeance than that. He gathered his men at Kiev and marched them south to the Tartar fortress. No one saw them come; not a footfall was heard. A sharp-eyed sentry scanning the walls might have seen ants in their thousands creeping in a single, silent column underneath the iron gates, but no sentry saw. Only the Khan and his soldiers within the strong-walled fortress saw warriors spring up where tiny ants had been. In the moments that followed, the Tartars all died on Russian swords.

was the yew, for instance—so much a tree of death that nothing would grow in the shade of its boughs; and the willow, which pulled up its roots and shuffled whispering after travelers foolhardy enough to venture out at night when the owl called and the ferret and other creatures hunted. The tall trees grew in multitudes so dense that in England, it was said, a squirrel could hop from Land's End to the Roman Wall without touching the ground.

Few dared that wilderness except the wizards. They, like the sweet singer Taliesin and the battle-brave Gwydion, were armed with words. Gwydion's name, in fact, meant "to speak poetry"—the man himself defined in terms of the powers of his speech—and every story about him shows the sway his words held over the things of the earth, both when he was young and roisterous, and later, when he grew in wisdom and kindness.

Gwydion lived in Gwynedd, in northern Wales, the nephew and heir to Math the Ancient, Gwynedd's ruler and himself a fearsome wizard. Math taught Gwydion profound enchantments, and he schooled the younger man in the right use of his powers.

It was a hard schooling, but it was one Gwydion required, for he used his fledgling skills carelessly, so that they made evil ends. It happened that Math had a handmaiden named Goewin, who never left his side except when he went to battle. Gwydion's brother Gilfaethwy desired the maiden, but there seemed no way he could approach her. He began to languish, growing pale and wan. To help him, Gwydion settled on the simple expedient of starting a war, thereby drawing Math from Goewin's side.

Accordingly, he took Gilfaethwy, along with a company of young warriors disguised as bards, to the south of Wales. The lord of this region, Pryderi, had a herd of wonderful swine—a gift, it was said, from the lord of the underworld, Arawn himself. At Pryderi's court, the youths were received joyfully, as bards always were. There was a feast, and Gwydion delighted the assembly with his songs and tales. In return, he asked Pryderi for a boon: the fabulous swine.

"That I cannot do," replied Pryderi, "for I have the beasts on the promise that I will neither sell nor give them away."

"You cannot sell or give them," Gwydion said slyly, "but that does not prevent you from exchanging them for something that is better."

It was so, and Pryderi agreed. Gwydion promised to offer an exchange the next day. That night he looked around him for the raw stuff of illusion and found it in a group of toadstools. He stared at them and, with the spells he knew, urged them into new forms. Soon, instead of parasols of fungus, there stood before Gwydion twelve mighty black stallions, their backs overlaid with mantles of scarlet trimmed in gold, and twelve black greyhounds with white breasts, whose collars and leashes were made of hide studded with gold, and twelve golden shields.

The glittering ruse was a success: Pryderi gave up the pigs. Gwydion and his company set out as quickly as they could

for home, since an illusion of that sort lasted one day only.

Soon Pryderi saw his hounds and horses shrink to toadstools. He set off with his forces in pursuit. In Gwynedd, against Math's greater numbers, Pryderi's men were massacred. To spare the remnants of his company, Pryderi fought Gwydion in single combat and died.

Amid the noise and uproar, when Math was occupied with battle, Gilfaethwy sought out Goewin and raped her. It was a wicked deed and a mad one: Math, who could hear any whisper in the world, would surely find out.

He did, and he caused Gwydion and Gilfaethwy to come to his fortress, Caer Dathyl, to make reparation for the men and animals lost in the foolish battle, for the needless death of Pryderi and for the shame of Goewin. Each year, for three successive years, Math changed the young men into a different pair of beasts: hind and stag, boar and sow, wolf and she-wolf. The worst indignity, fine payment for the nature of the crime, was this: That each year for three years the pair must mate — taking turns as the female — and produce offspring, so that when finally Math relented and restored the brothers to human form, there were three new living creatures to remind the brothers of how they had offended nature.

Gwydion's transgression was thus engraved on his heart. Later he became known as a saver, a restorer and even a giver of life. Appropriately, the materials he worked with were growing things. The humble mushrooms of his careless youth gave way to other plants — to trees and healing herbs, to seaweeds such as kelp and red dulse, and once, in the great venture of his life, to the flowers of oak, meadowsweet and broom (*pages 46-47*).

*C*uriously enough, among all the stories of Gwydion's deeds — his songs and spells, his shape-shifting and illusion-making — none survives to show him as a weather-worker. But he must have been, for mastery of the elements was the mark of the enchanter then as later. In times of peace, the sailor's helping winds, the farmer's slanting rains and smiling summer sun all worked, it was said, at wizards' will. In times of war, the people turned to those who could make of wind and water either swords or shields.

Grim weatherworking stories trickled down from icy, wind-swept Finland. Vainamöinen suffered from the weaknesses of age: He sometimes lacked important parts of spells and, sadder still, he never obtained a wife, for Joukahainen's sister Aino drowned herself rather than marry such an elder. Still, he was fairly called the Steadfast, for he never ceased to defend the people of his region — the Kaleva — from their enemy to the north.

This was the sorceress Louhi, mistress of a land called Pohjola and an implacable adversary. At various times she sent darkness and plagues to the Kaleva, but Vainamöinen's magic always provided protection against them. Louhi sought the prosperity of the Finns, and for a time she had it: Much of it rested in a magical mill called the Sampo, which had been made by a Finn and which Louhi obtained by

With Ilmarinen and Lemminkäinen at his side, Vainamöinen the Steadfast fought the storm-spells and taloned anger of Louhi, Sorceress of the North.

Guardian of the Isle of Man, Manannan Mac Lir rode a horse called Enbarr, meaning "Splendid Mane," that took him with ease over land or sea. No weapon could pierce Manannan's armor, and no enemy could survive his sword's thrust; that sword was called the Answerer.

a series of bribes and broken promises. When she refused to share its endless supplies of grain and gold, Vainamöinen, old as he was, went in quest of it; he was determined to repossess the precious mill through trickery.

The storytellers say that Vainamöinen took a company of men and sailed across the bay that divided his lands from Louhi's. When he reached her shores, he began to play his harp and to sing, and the dulcet music sent the land to sleep: No birds called, no beasts lowed, and Louhi and her soldiers lay entranced.

It was then an easy enough task to take the mill from the cave in which it was hidden, and set sail for home. For three days Vainamöinen and his crew sailed swiftly. And then the ship was enveloped in an impenetrable, lightless fog. The pilot could not steer. Louhi, it was clear, had awakened and discovered her loss, for this was not a natural fog.

Old Vainamöinen saved them: Muttering his spells, he slashed the fog to ribbons with his sword and scattered it like feathers into the sky.

At once the winds began to howl and the waves to billow as storms settled upon the Finns and their precious cargo. But the old man's magic held fast, and he thrust the storms—more sendings from the sorceress—back into the sea.

In the end, Louhi herself came after Vainamöinen, in the shape of a monstrous, ravening sea bird. She settled on the mast of the ship, darkening the sky with her wings. Then there was fierce battle. The wizard fought the sorceress with his sword and, when he had to, with his bare hands, until she was torn and bleeding. Defeated, she flew limping to her own lands, leaving the remains of the mill—for parts of it had been lost during the battle—to Vainamöinen and his people.

No greater contrast to those doleful Northern battle sagas could be found than in the stories of that insouciant and most beloved weather wizard, Manannan Mac Lir, across the world on his wave-washed Isle of Man.

Manannan sprang from the ancient Irish race, the Tuatha de Danann, who, long before history began, retreated into invisibility, leaving the country to mere mortals. Manannan's special domain was the sea, where his power was supreme, and innumerable legends surround his name: He had, it is said, a boat that knew his destination without prompting and traveled there without the help of sail or oar. In armor that shone as brightly as the sun, he rode his horse over land or water; the mere sight of his sword caused the strength to drain from his enemies. And when he cloaked himself or any other person in his magic mantle, it extinguished them from view.

As long as he lived—some say he is living still—his kingdom was invulnerable. When enemies approached, he enveloped the island in mist, and they sailed by unaware. He could raise storms if he wanted; and if he needed to, he could toss wooden chips into the water and make each grow into a warship. He could conjure 100 armed men from each of his troops.

In peace he was a provider of prosperity. He cultivated fish as if they were cattle, and when the pigs from his herd were slaughtered, the bones re-formed themselves into plump, living beasts. He was the happiest and most generous of wizards, and he made happy those about him.

Manannan had a fatherly fondness for the Irish, a race he kept under a watchful eye. He trained the country's young warriors, provided them with powerful weapons and healed their battle wounds. Those who had acquaintance with him usually came out of it better, wiser men.

There was, for instance, the lesson he taught Cormac Mac Art. Cormac was a wise if somewhat pettish Irish king. The chink in his wisdom was his opinion of women. "Crabby, haughty, lewd, bird-brain," he described them. "Greedy, vindictive, niggardly, quick to insult, eloquent of trifles," and more in this vein.

One day as Cormac walked the ramparts of his wooden fortress at Tara, seat of Irish kings, he saw a young man approaching, carrying a silver branch from which nine golden apples hung.

The young man shook the branch, and the apples tinkled a sweet music.

The delicate melody of the apple bells made Cormac straightaway forget all cares. He hailed the young man and asked whether he would sell the apple branch.

"Surely," came the reply. "There is nothing I have I would not sell."

"And what is the price?"

In his youth, Merlin the Enchanter observed a duel of dragons and was inspired to prophecy.
He foresaw the rivers of England run red with the blood of battle; but he also
foresaw the coming of King Arthur and the glorious reign that followed.

"I will tell you when you undertake to buy," answered the young man.

The King agreed. "And what is the price?" he asked again.

"Your wife and children."

And whether it was the effect of the music or irritation with his wife, Cormac let the three go without protest.

A year later, despite the music of the apple bells, he found himself pining for his family. Driven by his loneliness, Cormac set out along the road they had taken. As he walked, a mist arose around him, and when it cleared, he found himself in a strange, dreamlike land, where buildings of satin and of feathers stood crookedly in green meadows. He walked until the day drew in, and finally he came to a brightly lighted palace. A man at the palace gate greeted him with high good humor and invited him to dine and rest.

Inside, a pig was ready for the spit. Cormac's host cut a quarter from the pig and set it to cook at a blazing fire.

"Now," said the host with a smile, "How shall we entertain ourselves? I'll tell you. Give us a tale. And mark this fact: If your tale is a true one, this quarter of the pig will be cooked by the end of it."

"I would sooner you told one first," said Cormac, "and then your wife, and I shall happily tell mine afterward."

"Very well," said his host gaily. "Guests must have their will and way. Here is my tale. I own seven of these pigs, but with those seven I can feed the whole world. When one is killed and eaten I put the bones back in the sty, and when the sun comes up it is live and whole again. Now, if I have told you the truth, the quarter will be done." He pierced the meat with his knife, and indeed it was.

His wife's turn came. "I have seven white cows," she said, "and the milk in them never runs dry. If all the people of the world were gathered in the plain, I could give them all to drink. And if I speak the truth, the second quarter will be done." And it was.

Now Cormac knew who his host was, for only Manannan owned such pigs and cows. He said so, and the wizard nodded, but called for Cormac's story without delay. Cormac told how he lost his wife and how he missed her, and by the time he finished, the third quarter of the pig was cooked. Manannan laughed.

"You are King Cormac," he said, "and I'll tell you the truth. It was I in that young man and I who took your family—fairly, remember, and according to the agreement we made. But you're here now, and thinking differently it seems, and I'm happy and honored to see you. As for your wife . . ." Here the wizard jumped up, strode to a darkly curtained door, threw it open and called the three inside to come out. They were Cormac's wife and children.

After the embraces and tears, they all sat down at a long oak table. Manannan took up a golden goblet.

"Now here's another curious thing," he said. "Speak a lie before this cup and it will break in a hundred pieces. Tell the truth and it's whole again."

"Show me," said Cormac.

"Very well, I will," replied Manannan, with a chuckle. "Since I took your wife

Protector of Britain's future, Merlin spirited the infant Arthur away from his
birthplace at the fortress of Tintagel. No one in power saw the young King until he
came to claim his crown, and Merlin never told where he had hidden the child.

away, I'm sorry to tell you, she has found a new husband." Cormac felt steel bands tighten in his chest. But Manannan laughed, and as he did, the noise was drowned by the clatter of golden fragments on the board.

"I'm afraid," said the wizard's wife demurely, "that my husband has lied." The pieces of the goblet flew together.

After that, the evening passed in stories that grew ever more fanciful. As Manannan elaborated, the cup, in pieces again, seemed to lose all will to restore itself. Eventually the company retired, but when Cormac awoke, he was in his own palace, his own dear wife asleep beside him and near the bed the golden goblet for truth and the silver branch of apples for delight. The misogynist had had a pointed lesson.

Manannan, wise and merry, song-filled Taliesin, Math and old Vainamöinen—all of them were, in a sense, forerunners, bearers of the flame that was to shine the steadiest at the last, in Merlin the Enchanter. It was as if Merlin—the name is a Latin rendering of the Celtic *Myrddin*—gathered into himself all their various powers to serve one purpose: the making of the last great kingdom of the old Britons. Of the innumerable legends surrounding him, that is the most enduring; one early name for Britain is, in fact, *Clas Myrddin*, meaning "Merlin's Enclosure."

Like the older wizards, the English Merlin attracted legends as nectar does bees, which makes the man himself extraordinarily elusive. The songs and predictions of two early Welsh Myrddins—one a bard

and companion of Taliesin, one a warrior driven to madness and prophecy by the horror of battle—usually were attached to him. And the mysterious and frightening giants' circle at Stonehenge was explained as his work: He is said to have transported the monoliths from the Irish mountain Killáire, an unlikely tale. These various stories are superfluous: The real matter of Merlin lies in two episodes.

Merlin's magic first came to light in this way: In war-racked Fifth Century Britain, by a series of villainies too tortuous to describe, a king called Vortigern had usurped the throne from its rightful heirs, two boys named Aurelius Ambrosius and Uther, who fled for safety to Brittany. Vortigern imported armies of vicious Saxon mercenaries to protect himself from his own unruly subjects, but these men took control of the country. The King thereupon retired to Snowdon in Wales, to build himself a stronghold.

The mighty tower Vortigern planned simply crumbled as he built it. Vortigern consulted his court magicians, who announced that if the mortar and stones were sprinkled with the blood of a boy who had no father, the building would hold. Accordingly, the King sent messengers throughout the countryside, seeking such a boy. In Carmarthen, in southern Wales, they found him, and took him with his mother to the King. She said that she never had lain with a man, but that a spirit had visited her at night and made her son.

Vortigern now had his sacrificial victim, but the boy, who was Merlin, forestalled him. He told the King that if he dug underneath the building site, he would find a

A realm in the balance

When Merlin first brought Arthur to his throne, the King was young and battle-proud. It happened that he challenged a knight named Pellinore — who was a petty king himself — to single combat. They jousted with lances, and Arthur was unhorsed; they dueled on foot with swords, and Pellinore won. Then Pellinore demanded that Arthur yield his knightly honor and surrender, but the King chose the death blow instead.

Just as Pellinore raised his battle sword to strike, Merlin appeared beside the men and thundered what he knew — that the hope of Britain lived in King Arthur and would die with him. Heeding these words, Pellinore stayed his hand.

Then Merlin told the King that the mighty knight he had fought, and the knight's sons as well, would become Arthur's faithful servants. And all this happened as Merlin foretold.

35

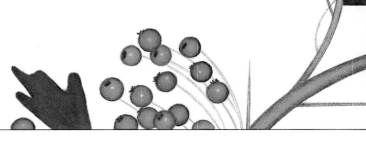

A blade for Britain's King

The time came early in Arthur's reign when Merlin told the King that his true sword awaited him. Together the British King and the Enchanter rode through forests and uplands until at last they came to a still mountain lake, where white swans cried softly through the mist.

At the verge of this lake floated a gilded boat. Arthur and Merlin stepped into it and, drawn by invisible hands, floated to the center of the waters. There, a hand broke through the mist, holding up the sword Excalibur, sheathed in a jeweled scabbard.

In silence, Arthur grasped the hilt. The sword would be his strength, for it was magically empowered; no enemy could defeat the King as long as he carried it, and the scabbard was an enchanted talisman against injury.

pool of water—which was the source of the building's unsteadiness—and if that pool was drained, two sleeping dragons would be revealed. The pool was drained, and all appeared as Merlin said. A red dragon and a white emerged from the pool and began to fight bitterly, while young Merlin sang his prophecies.

He told Vortigern that his end was near: The King, he said, would be slain either by marauding Saxons or by Aurelius and Uther, each of whom would succeed to the throne in turn. He predicted that the rivers of the country would run red with blood during the battles of the ensuing years as Briton fought Saxon, but that finally the Boar of Cornwall would trample the invaders and unite the country.

It happened just as Merlin foretold. The rightful heir, Aurelius, trapped Vortigern in one of his own towers and burned it to the ground. Aurelius, and in his turn Uther—now called Pendragon because his standard displayed a winged dragon—succeeded to the throne.

That was, in effect, the overture, the first notes of the magical strains that sang through the wizard Merlin. When the right

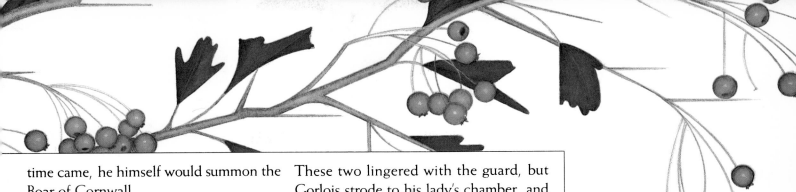

time came, he himself would summon the Boar of Cornwall.

The thing was set in motion in London, at Uther's coronation feast, when the King saw Igraine, wife of Gorlois of Cornwall, the most beautiful woman in Britain, and a fit mother of kings. Uther was entranced. His eyes flew continually to Igraine; he passed his own gold wine goblet to her; he lingered at her side.

Бis passion was obvious, and Gorlois, who loved his wife and would defy fate, was enraged. He took Igraine away at once and against Uther's order. He sequestered her in his castle of Tintagel, high on the wave-washed cliffs of Cornwall, and rode out on his lands to secure his other strongholds against Uther's army, which he knew would soon arrive.

Uther followed hotly, raiding and burning and intent on Igraine. He could not reach Tintagel, however: It was impregnable from the sea and reachable from the land only by a narrow isthmus of rock, well guarded. Uther sent for Merlin, who came, knowing what the King would ask, and determined on the act that would bring the savior of Britain.

The King did ask. Igraine, as Merlin knew, had become his heart's desire. More than that, it was clear that Uther's passion was consuming him.

The next night, the guard posted at the windy gates of Tintagel was amazed to see his lord, Gorlois, whom he thought to be fortifying his camp at Dimilioc to the southwest. With Gorlois were his friend Jordan and one of his captains, Britaelis.

These two lingered with the guard, but Gorlois strode to his lady's chamber, and there he stayed throughout the night.

In the small hours of the morning, the three men left Tintagel, and as the gray dawn broke, their true shapes returned to them. The false Gorlois was Uther, the man Jordan was an adviser of Uther's named Ulfin, and as for Britaelis, he was watchful Merlin, who had shifted all their shapes to bring about that one night's union safely. Gorlois died that same night, killed at Dimilioc by Uther's troops; and Igraine then married Uther. Nine months after the night, Igraine bore a son—Arthur, the Boar of Cornwall.

Times were perilous then, as Uther fought the Saxons and the northern tribes, not to mention the unruly factions among his own people. Merlin, aware of the dangers, had demanded of Uther a price for his aid: The wizard insisted on caring for Igraine's child. Thus, shortly after the birth, Merlin appeared at Tintagel again, and left by the postern gate, carrying the infant down the steep path through the cliffs to the sea below.

Nothing was seen of the boy for fifteen years. Some say that Merlin took him to Brittany, others that the wizard put the boy in the care of a knight named Ector in a safely remote part of England. In any case, Merlin saw that Arthur was protected and properly schooled, so that when the time came and Uther lay dying, Arthur was ready to take his rightful crown.

This is the story of the wizard, not the King, and it is not the place to tell of Arthur's long reign, of the battles he fought to forge his nation and of the treachery of

The hawthorn, covered with flowers in the spring and berries in the autumn, was considered a barrier against evil.

his nephew that ended its bright splendor. Merlin was there, just out of sight and watchful almost to the end, which he foresaw but was helpless to avert. It was he who found Arthur's sword, Excalibur, with the Lady of the Lake, and he who directed the construction of the Round Table.

But Merlin left before the end. By some accounts, he retreated to an invisible glass palace on an island, said to be Bardsey, off the Welsh coast.

He took for safekeeping—until they were needed—Britain's Thirteen Treasures: the Sword of Rhydderch, which poured forth invincible flame in the hands of a brave man; the Hamper of Gwyddno Long-Shank, which turned food for one into food for a hundred; the Horn of Brân, a supplier of endless drink; the Chariot of Morgan, which went anywhere the rider wished; the Halter of Clydno Eiddyn, which summoned the best of horses; the powerful knife of Llawfrodedd the Horseman; the Caldron of Dyrnwch, which cooked only for the brave; the Whetstone of Tudwal Tudglyd, which sharpened swords only for heroes; the Coat of Padarn Red-Coat, which fit only the wellborn; the Crock and Dish of Rhygenydd, which gave any food demanded; the Golden Chessboard of Gwenddolau, whose silver men played by themselves; and the Mantle of Arthur, which made its wearer invisible.

There are other accounts of Merlin's disappearance. It is said that he fell in love with a princess—or a fairy—whose name is variously given as Nimue, Niniane or Vivian. She learned his magical charms and with them locked the enchanter in a crystal cave—or a hawthorn bush or an oak tree in the forests in Brittany or a rocky tomb or in the air—where he lives invisible, having spoken only to tell Arthur's knight Sir Gawain about the Holy Grail.

The truth cannot be determined and does not matter. What matters is that Merlin, like the great enchanters before him, disappeared but did not die. Manannan retreated into invisibility, but kept watch over the Isle of Man, so that even in later times, sailors invoked his aid. Old Vainamöinen sailed in a copper boat to a place, his people said, between the upper reaches of the world and the lower reaches of the heavens, leaving his magic harp behind.

So the first wizards left the earth, disappearing into a silent limbo, to wait for the time when their countries might call them again. For the world was changing. The numinous powers abroad in its young age gradually receded, but piecemeal, like retreating ice, leaving small pockets of influence all over the earth. Man retreated, too, away from nature and into himself.

none of this happened all at once; indeed, people with some of the first wizards' powers lived many centuries after Merlin. But the climate had retreated from magic. Those who dared to deal with ineffable powers would come to dryly classify and regulate what magical resources they could unearth, and codes and registers are always the enemies of spontaneous activity. The age of earthy wizard heroes gave way to that of the scholars of sorcery, people who tampered with powers no longer naturally theirs—and paid the price of curiosity.

At the end of his life—if this tale is true—the last of the great enchanters did not die.
Some say that Merlin yielded to the blandishments of a fairy and slept, and she housed him
in a tree, to rest in safety until called to aid his countrymen once more.

The Welsh Enchanter's Fosterling

The rich mountain lands of Gwynedd, in northern Wales, lay under the protection of the wizards Math and Gwydion, two men whose deeds became the subject of many a song. Their most renowned adventure—the one that made the saddest tale—began at Caer Dathyl, Math's mountain fortress. The adventure was brought about by haughty Arianrod, Gwydion's sister and a sorceress in her own right.

Arianrod came to Caer Dathyl to serve as Math's handmaiden, thereby bringing shame upon her own head, for only virgins held that honor and Arianrod clearly was no virgin. On the day she arrived she bore two sons. (No one knew who the father was, and she never told.) She abandoned them at once and fled to her palace by the sea.

One infant leaped like a fish into the water and disappeared, but Gwydion caught up the other, and he became a father to the child. He saw to it that the boy was tenderly cared for, and he anxiously surrounded the frail life with protective charms, so that as the years passed, the child grew precociously strong and healthy.

When the boy was four (yet as tall as a child of eight), it came time for his naming:

His birth had been strange as it was, and lacking a name, he would be nothing. In Gwynedd at that time, only a mother could name her child, so Gwydion set off with the boy for Arianrod's seagirt palace.

Arianrod welcomed her brother Gwydion civilly enough, but when she discovered that the child with him was her son—living proof of her humiliation and exile—she turned on the pair, sparkling with fury.

"I will swear this fate on him," she said in her silvery voice, "that he shall have no name until he obtains one from me. And I shall never give it."

"That is a wicked oath, and you are a wicked woman," replied her brother grimly. "But the boy shall have a name all the same." And he turned on his heel and left the palace, taking the boy with him.

Some days later, a tidy little ship sailed into the harbor below Arianrod's castle and tied up at the wharf. The ship carried traveling shoemakers, and the shoes they made were of gilded Spanish leather, wonders in-

movement quicker than her eye could follow, the boy brought down the bird with a stone. It was beautifully done. Arianrod laughed and clapped her hands. She cried, "Oh, well shot, Fair-haired Skillful Hand."

At once the ship and shoes vanished. Where the ship had been, only seaweed floated, and on the wharf stood Gwydion and Arianrod's son. Gwydion smiled: "The boy has a name, and a good one. Lleu Llaw Gyffes he shall be." For those were the words she had spoken in Welsh.

Arianrod stiffened as she recognized the trick. "Very well," she said coldly, "here is

deed, and fit for a queen. Arianrod commanded shoes for herself when she heard of this, but the answer came that none could be made for her unless she herself went down to the shoemakers. She did that.

On the deck of the ship she found only an old shoemaker and his yellow-haired apprentice, stitching away at the gleaming leather. As she gave them good day, a tiny wren lighted on the head of the mast. With a

another fate, then. The boy shall have no weapons until I arm him myself. And I shall never arm him."

But Gwydion only laughed, saluted his sister and left her. He took Lleu away to a fortress to the north called Dinas Dinlleu.

The years passed quietly for Lleu. In the fields and woods around Dinas Dinlleu, he learned to handle even the most fiery horses; he became a skillful archer and swordsman. Under Gwydion's care, he grew tall and straight and golden, the image of a fine lord. But because of Arianrod's oath, he could not bear arms and take his place as a man among men, and he drew away by himself. Gwydion saw this, and knew the time had come to act.

One night, two bards appeared at Arianrod's palace by the sea. She welcomed them, as was proper treatment for bards, and feasted them handsomely. The evening passed peacefully, with songs and tales.

In the morning, however, the palace was roused by trumpet calls. From the windows could be seen a mighty fleet of warships, their sails so full and crowding that they hid the surface of the sea.

Terrified, Arianrod and her maidens ran to the room where the bards slept, seeking help (bards, after all, were wise and powerful men). These two carried no weapons, but Arianrod had weapons brought from her own strongrooms. Her maidens armed one of the men and she armed the other, strapping on his belt and scabbard, buckling his helmet, handing him his shield.

As soon as she had finished, the ships disappeared: Nothing was seen beyond the shore but gentle waves, nothing heard but the cries of the gulls. And in the palace, too, a change had occurred. In place of the bards stood Gwydion and Arianrod's son, who bore the arms she herself had given him. Gwydion was smiling.

Then Arianrod swore her final oath: "This man will have no wife from any race on earth at this time." So Arianrod sealed the fate of Lleu Llaw Gyffes. It was a fearful oath, condemning Arianrod's son to a solitary bed and worse: Without a wife, Lleu would be set apart from other men; without a wife, he would be torn from the pattern of nature, with no children to bear his name.

This was a grave business, and what Gwydion did next was more solemn than conjuring illusions and shifting shape to trick an enemy. He needed stronger magic than even he controlled, and so he went to Math at Caer Dathyl. Math was Gwydion's uncle; he had taught Gwydion lovingly. When Gwydion arrived, Math was waiting: He heard every word whispered and he knew Gwydion needed his powers.

Almost nothing is known of how the two

enchanters worked. They called for masses of flowers—oak, meadowsweet and broom. They retired to the inner recesses of Caer Dathyl, and it is said that the spells and charms they conjured with were graver than most wizards dared to utter.

When they emerged, the flowers had become a maiden. She sprang to life full grown, sweet and fragrant as April and May and more beautiful than any human woman. They named her Blodeuwedd, or "Flower Face," and gave her to Lleu.

Thus Gwydion made the boy Lleu Llaw Gyffes into a man, who bore a proper man's arms and had better than a proper man's wife. Math gave Lleu the lands called Ardudwy in southern Gwynedd, with their fortress at Mur Castell, so Lleu also had a man's work to do. He went there with his flower wife, and Gwydion rested, content.

The factor that none of them reckoned with was Blodeuwedd.

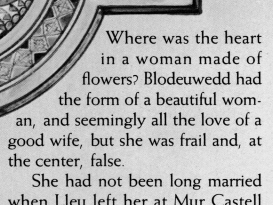

Where was the heart in a woman made of flowers? Blodeuwedd had the form of a beautiful woman, and seemingly all the love of a good wife, but she was frail and, at the center, false.

She had not been long married when Lleu left her at Mur Castell while he journeyed to the court of Math, and on that same day, she saw a hunting party coursing a stag across her lands. All through the afternoon, while Blodeuwedd watched from her castle wall, the hunters appeared and disappeared among the trees, and at last, at twilight, she heard the shouts that heralded the kill.

In an hour, the hunters were at her gates. Blodeuwedd offered them shelter so that they would not have to ride to their own lands in the dark. Their leader was Goronwy, Lord of Penllyn, whose territory bordered her own. Goronwy was called the Handsome because of the dashing figure he cut, and his fine looks were her downfall. When Blodeuwedd saw him in her hall, she was filled with passion. She made Goronwy her lover that night, and afterward could not bear to be without him.

As for Goronwy, he was a man without honor. He wanted Blodeuwedd and he wanted the rich lands of Ardudwy as well. But he knew, as everyone in Gwynedd knew, that Lleu was under Gwydion's protection. He soon left Blodeuwedd for his own lands. Before Goronwy left her, however, he told her what she must do to have him again.

Lleu returned from serving Math and Gwydion to find his pretty wife silent and pensive. In the night, she turned away from him to weep.

"What is this?" he asked in surprise.

She replied, "When you were away, I thought of you, and feared you would die before me, leaving me here alone."

This was touching and—considering the safeguards Gwydion had placed on him in childhood—absurd. To calm his wife, Lleu said, "Unless God strikes me down, it would be a hard task for anyone to kill me."

Blodeuwedd began to plead: "If you can be killed at all, tell me. My knowledge of the danger will be your shield."

Then Lleu out of love told what should have remained a secret between him and Gwydion. "First, there is the spear: I can be killed only by him who makes the spear itself, and he must labor on it for a year, working only on holy days. And even if the spear were made, I would be safe, for I cannot be killed in a house or out of doors, I cannot be killed when I am on horseback or on foot, I cannot be killed on dry land or in the water." Thus Lleu reassured Blodeuwedd the flower-faced.

"Then there is no place you can die," said Blodeuwedd. "Or is there a place?"

There was a place, and Lleu told Blodeuwedd where. In those days, people made special baths. Caldrons were placed near rivers for the fresh water and roofed to keep off the rain. If Lleu stood with one foot on the rim of such a bath and the other foot off the ground—on the back, say, of a goat—all the requirements for his death would be fulfilled: He would be in a borderline place, neither indoors nor out, neither on dry land nor in the water, neither on horseback nor on foot. Blodeuwedd laughed and asked no

more. Lleu thought this was because he had soothed her fear, but the messenger she sent in the morning to Goronwy, waiting in his fortress at Penllyn, knew better.

A year passed peacefully in Ardudwy. Blodeuwedd remained just the same to Lleu: She still was sweet and fragrant and loving, and he was happy. But off in Penllyn, Goronwy spent his time working on the spear.

In a year, the spear was finished, long and straight and tipped with poison. Goronwy carried it secretly to the very walls of Mur Castell, and in secret he sent word to Blodeuwedd that he was there and ready.

Blodeuwedd was ready, too: Her long waiting was almost over. She went to Lleu and said in her pretty way, "If I have a bath built, will you show me how you would tempt the fates?"

Lleu said yes. What harm could come from a wife so childlike and so flower-like? And harm might come from playing the coward before such a wife.

The bath was built on the banks of the River Gynvael. Blodeuwedd led Lleu there and watched while he bathed. Other eyes watched too: Goronwy hid with the spear in the shadows across the river. When Lleu rose from the bath, Blodeuwedd was there, offering the back of a goat to stand on. He indulged her: He put one foot on the rim of the bath and one on the goat's back, and in that instant, Goronwy cast the spear from the shadows. The shaft broke with the blow, but the head pierced Lleu's side. He gave a great cry of pain and shot one look at his wife. Then he disappeared. Where he had been, there stood a great wounded golden eagle. It rose into the air, wheeled and vanished into the mountains. Goronwy and Blodeuwedd paid no heed. Their waiting was over, and they returned to Mur Castell. Goronwy took the fortress, as he did the woman, for his own. In the days that followed, he and his companions subdued all of Ardudwy, so that he had those lands as well as those at Penllyn. It was not very long

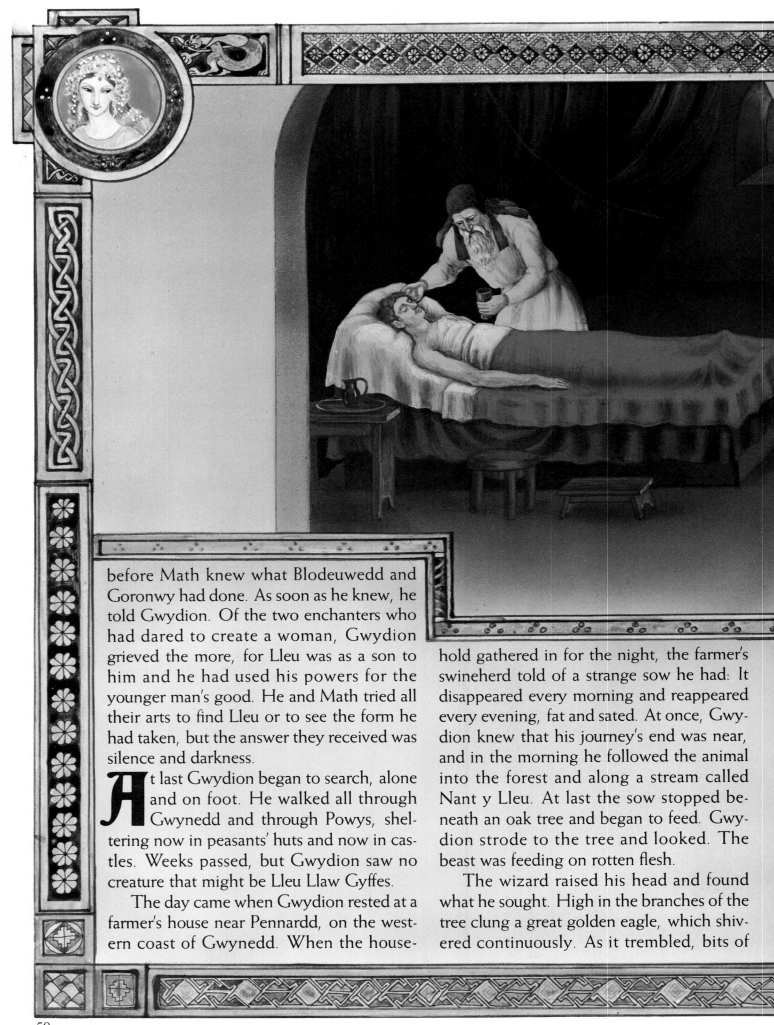

before Math knew what Blodeuwedd and Goronwy had done. As soon as he knew, he told Gwydion. Of the two enchanters who had dared to create a woman, Gwydion grieved the more, for Lleu was as a son to him and he had used his powers for the younger man's good. He and Math tried all their arts to find Lleu or to see the form he had taken, but the answer they received was silence and darkness.

At last Gwydion began to search, alone and on foot. He walked all through Gwynedd and through Powys, sheltering now in peasants' huts and now in castles. Weeks passed, but Gwydion saw no creature that might be Lleu Llaw Gyffes.

The day came when Gwydion rested at a farmer's house near Pennardd, on the western coast of Gwynedd. When the household gathered in for the night, the farmer's swineherd told of a strange sow he had: It disappeared every morning and reappeared every evening, fat and sated. At once, Gwydion knew that his journey's end was near, and in the morning he followed the animal into the forest and along a stream called Nant y Lleu. At last the sow stopped beneath an oak tree and began to feed. Gwydion strode to the tree and looked. The beast was feeding on rotten flesh.

The wizard raised his head and found what he sought. High in the branches of the tree clung a great golden eagle, which shivered continuously. As it trembled, bits of

flesh fell from it to the foot of the tree.

Gwydion sat on the ground. The sow snuffled beneath the tree and the wind sighed in the branches, but the eagle made not a sound. The wizard gazed at it thoughtfully for some moments. Then he sang a charm. The bird slipped down to the middle branches of the tree. Gwydion paused; he sang another charm, and then he waited. The feeble creature dropped to a lower branch. And a third time, Gwydion sang, bidding the bird to come to him. When he finished, the eagle dropped to Gwydion's knee.

At once he struck the bird and it van-ished. Before the wizard lay Lleu Llaw Gyffes. The bones were starting from the young man's flesh, and he had a great wound in his side. But Lleu was alive.

There followed a time of healing and waiting. Gwydion took Lleu to Math at Caer Dathyl, and the two enchanters set to work. They used the herbs of the forest and their own incantations, as well as the skills of all their physicians. Between them, they healed the young man.

In the period of healing, the men of Gwynedd began to arm and leave their strongholds and their farms. Across the hills and through the forests they came, gather-ing at the call of Math and Gwydion. The enchanters raised a mighty force to capture the false bride and her lover.

After the months of healing, the day

came when Lleu's body was strong again. But his heart hurt him, and at last he said the word the wizards waited for. He went to Math and told him, "Lord, the time has come for me to seek retribution for the evil that was done me."

Then Lleu and Gwydion led the host of Gwynedd toward Ardudwy, where Goronwy and Blodeuwedd were. The train of men and horses and chariots could be seen for miles, winding through the mountains, pennants fluttering and spears flashing. The news of their coming was not long in reaching Goronwy and Blodeuwedd.

The pair knew they were lost: Their small forces were no match for the host of Gwynedd, and they had no means to battle the might of Gwydion and, behind Gwydion, Math. They could only run. Goronwy, always false, rode away to his own lands in Penllyn, leaving his mistress behind. Blodeuwedd ran for her life, fearing her creator's wrath. She left Mur Castell on foot, heading into the mountains to hide

as an animal would do, and she took her maidens along with her.

So Lleu and Gwydion captured the fortress at Mur Castell with ease. Gwydion did not linger there. He set off after his creature Blodeuwedd, moving steadily up the winding mountain paths, never rushing and never pausing, but always gaining on the fleeing group of women as they stumbled along high crags and on the cliffs that bordered a deep mountain lake. The women saw him as a speck far below, now lost to sight, now appearing. Each time he appeared, he was closer, and in their terror they continually looked behind them to gauge Gwydion's progress.

And their fear was their undoing. One by one, they lost their footing and fell screaming through the air down into the icy mountain lake. At last no one was left but Blodeuwedd, who had led them all to their deaths. She panted on alone, scrambling through the dirt, not flower-like now. And at her back she always heard the wizard,

making his inexorable way up the mountain behind her, moving neither fast nor slow.

At last Blodeuwedd could go no farther; she could only wait. Some minutes passed before Gwydion appeared. He contemplated the woman he had made and he said, "I will not kill you. There are worse fates. I will let you go in the form of a bird. But for the shame you brought on Lleu, you shall be a bird that never shows its face in the light of day, a predator hated by other birds. You will always hunt alone." He raised his hand, and in place of Blodeuwedd stood a taloned owl.

"You will not lose your name," added Gwydion before he turned to leave. And indeed, in Wales the owl would always

be known as blodeuwedd, or "flower face."

Gwydion returned to Mur Castell, where Lleu was in command, and together they waited for the messenger they knew would come from their enemy: Goronwy was unlikely to risk their invading Penllyn. A herald finally arrived, asking what Lleu would take as payment for the crime. The herald carried back this word from Lleu: "Tell Goronwy that this is the least I will accept: He must stand where I stood when he cast the spear. I will stand where he stood and cast the spear at him as he did at me."

When Goronwy heard this, he turned to his kinsmen and said, "Will no one take the blow in my stead?" It was the custom in Wales that leaders had champions who stood for them to spare the kingdom's princes. But there was no man who would stand for the dishonorable Goronwy. Only silence answered him.

He traveled to the River Gynvael, where Lleu waited. He stood where Lleu had, and Lleu raised the spear. But Goronwy cried, "Lord grant me a boon. A woman brought me to this pass. For that I beg you, let me hold a stone between me and the blow."

"I will not refuse you," said Lleu, a generous man, and he stayed his hand while Goronwy lifted a stone that lay on the riverbank and clasped it before his body like a shield. Then Lleu cast. The spear shot through the air, straight to its mark, piercing the stone and the body of Goronwy, so that his back broke and he died.

So Lleu was avenged. The years went by and Math was, it was said, succeeded by Gwydion and then by Lleu. The stone that Goronwy had used for a shield, pierced with its hole, was still to be seen hundreds of years later, and it was called the Stone of Goronwy. The place of the spear throw was called the Hill of the Battle.

In dusty scrolls and antique charts, Roger Bacon found the keys to wizardly power.

Chapter Two

Masters of Forbidden Arts

For an outsider, the odds of finding a particular volume within the chambers of the Oxford scholar Roger Bacon would have been close to those related to the retrieval of a needle from a stack of hay. Books were everywhere, spread on sturdy oak chests, packed in solid ranks on window seats, piled in pillars on the floor.

They were not, of course, printed books: Gutenberg would not construct his press for another 200 years. These were massive works of art, lovingly lettered on crisp parchment or thick vellum, gleaming with gold leaf, bound in satiny leather and annotated in Bacon's own monkish hand, arched and pointed as a Gothic church. The rarer ones were chained in place. There were codices of Aristotle's philosophies and commentaries on them by the Roman scholar Boethius. The *Picatrix*, a curious compilation of Arabic magical theories, was there, as well as the

Canon of Medicine by the Persian physician Avicenna, parts of which dealt with secret arts. Nearby lay *The Key of Solomon*, Bacon's manuscript copy of the Hebrew King's formulas and spells (preserved for centuries by the Arabs, these had passed through Moorish Spain and thence to the wizards of northern Europe).

Bacon's own works, in various stages of completion – his Greek and Hebrew grammars, his *General Principles of Natural Philosophy* – were scattered about, too, along with the materials for writing them. He had quires of ivory vellum, the leaves already neatly folded to make the book divisions called quaternions. He had a knife for scraping the surface of the sheets and pumice for smoothing them, boxwood rulers for marking margins and a little pot of hot coals for drying the ink on the page. And he had feathery goose and crow quills and jars of oak bark steeped in water for the making of ink. Besides the paraphernalia of reading and writing – not to mention such articles of living as candles and oil lamps and hourglasses – there was a litter of other objects, the gear and tackle and trim of dozens of

trades that signified Bacon's insatiable and wide-ranging curiosity. Scattered among the books were various lenses and prisms for examining the refractions of light and the colors of the rainbow; a camera obscura for watching eclipses; a beaded abacus; gleaming brass compasses, alidades, quadrants and astrolabes for the observation of the heavens; white skeletons of birds for studying the mechanisms of flight; and the flasks, bell jars, crucibles and retorts of the practicing alchemist.

The general effect on Bacon's visitors was one of bookish chaos. They were therefore amazed at the speed with which he located any volume he wanted amidst his coverlet of opened tomes. If he sought a fact or confirmation of a theory, he knew which line, which page, which book, which pile or shelf and which zone of his study to find it in. He did so with such deftness that it looked like sleight of hand and added weight to the whispers about Bacon's practices and powers — whispers that had spread beyond the dreaming spires of Oxford to Paris and Bologna, where other scholars worked. Even though he was a Franciscan and supposedly unlikely to traffic with any but holy powers, tales of wizardry gathered about his name.

Bacon's skills with magic, it was said, were known at the royal court — indeed, had been witnessed by the King himself. Chroniclers told how this was so.

One day, as the friar worked in his chambers, a knock sounded at the door. At Bacon's command, it creaked open, admitting a dignified young man whose surcoat bore the badge of the Plantagenet kings and whose shoes displayed the gro-

Satan was always ready to enter into a dark alliance with wizards, knowing he would benefit in the end. The fiend form was just one guise; he could also appear as man or animal

58

tesquely exaggerated toes that marked the man of fashion.

The young man regarded the friar's cluttered, musty rooms with distaste and gave his message curtly. King Edward, he announced, was at the Oxfordshire house of a nobleman. Being nearby, he wished to see a demonstration of Bacon's powers.

The friar assented. As the royal messenger turned to go, however, Bacon remarked, "I shall depart here after you but arrive two hours before you."

Since the distance was just five miles and the messenger's horse a spirited steed compared with the friar's mule, the young man only shrugged.

"And another thing," Bacon added with a wicked smile. "I could name the wench you lay with last night. Indeed, I shall, later in the day."

The messenger merely replied that all scholars were liars, and he took himself off. Bacon smiled again, recited a spell and in very short order presented himself at the castle where the King presided.

The King welcomed the friar graciously to the castle's great hall, complimented him on his learning and asked for a show of his magic. Bacon at first demurred with becoming modesty, saying that there were many greater than he. Still, in the service of his monarch he was prepared to use what poor powers he possessed.

He produced the wizard's wand of hazelwood from the folds of his voluminous habit. The King and Queen and the lords and ladies of the court formed a chattering ring around the friar to watch him work.

Bacon raised the wand. From the stones of the walls and floor, from the fabric of the tapestries, from the beams of the ceiling, there swelled a wonderful sound, a distillation of plain song and canticle, of aubade and serenade, a braided ribbon of harmonies so delicately sweet that it enchanted the ear, and so perfectly thoughtful that it gave the heart ease. It was an echo of the music of the spheres, the song the planets sang as they whirled in their unerring courses. It filled the air. The courtiers ceased to chatter.

The sound diminished, and Bacon said quietly, "That was to please Your Graces' sense of hearing. The rest is for your other senses." He raised the wand again.

The music grew and changed in character, taking on the measured merriment of earthly dances. And five dancers appeared in the hall, first faint as shadows, then firm and real. Once fully materialized, they seemed a coarse contrast to the music: A court fool and a laundress danced a jig, while a bent figure in the skullcap and black robe of the usurer hovered near them, importuning. A footman appeared, a sneer on his lips and wrinkled hose upon his wiry shanks. He waved the moneylender away, toward a dandified chevalier, plump and mustachioed.

As they danced, however, the dancers altered. Scorn, greed and vanity left them, and they seemed, in the patterns of the dance, to transcend the meanness of their pursuits. Their bodies grew lithe and agile, and they reeled, somersaulted and pirouetted, sprang like dolphins from the water, flew like birds that ride the winds. At last, still dancing, they rose like a column of

With an artful wizardry, Roger Bacon shaped the formless air: He filled a palace with music and from the
harmonies fashioned dancers and a dance—an illusion that was only a pretty gift he made to please his kin

smoke into the air and vanished from view.

The dancers had risen, it seemed, to the realm of stars, far above the soul's sublunary prison, but the music of the masque continued, the only sound in the now-silent hall. The courtiers stood entranced, motionless as rows of statues; the King's hunting hounds lay still and quiet; his hawks drooped on their perches. At a window rested a butterfly, wings clasped, fast asleep.

Bacon raised his wand again and there grew from the floor of the hall a long trestle table, laden with peaches and pomegranates, strawberries, apricots and raspberries, gifts of the earth to please a king's taste. The friar flourished the wand once more and conjured from the air a nosegay of scents, the fragrances entwined with the music to make arpeggios of geranium and chords of roses and violets. Then into the eddying currents of sound, smell and taste, the wizard introduced a pleasure for the sense of touch: Weaving their way through the throng of spellbound courtiers came a troop of merchants, dressed in the bulky coats of Muscovy and Cathay, and bearing piles of silken furs, a ransom's worth of ermine and sable and fox.

At last, tucking his wand away, Bacon folded his arms into the sleeves of his habit and waited. The furriers wound their way out of the hall, the fruits trembled and dissolved into invisibility, the scents faded to a lingering memory of fragrance and the music to a single note, hovering in the air like the last frail echo of a silver bell.

King and courtiers slowly came to life, blinking and murmuring. The hounds lolloped whining to their feet. The hawks shuffled sideways on their perches so that the small bells attached to their jesses tinkled dully. The butterfly at the window quivered, then took flight.

At that moment, the King's messenger stumbled into the hall in a pitiful state indeed. As chroniclers relate, he was "all bedirted," his fine surcoat torn and soaking and his pretty pointed shoes crusted with mud. His horse, unaccountably heedless of the rein, had taken him on a demented gallop through every ditch, quagmire and stream in the county, and he was very angry. The ladies twitched their skirts out of harm's way as he passed.

He confronted Bacon furiously, sputtering about devils, but the friar said only, "I am here before you, as I promised. And, of course, I also promised to help you to your sweetheart, did I not?" He strode to an archway and pulled aside the curtain that covered it. Framed in the arch stood a kitchen maid, bulb-cheeked, grease-flecked, buxom and blushing. She clutched a basting ladle.

"Take care next time how you call scholars liars," said the friar. He bowed to the King and left a scene of dawning hilarity, the King and courtiers laughing, the poor kitchen maid clumsily curtseying and the messenger stammering an explanation of the presence of his latest, lowly conquest.

Although more frivolous in purpose, Bacon's illusion was no different in kind from the fleets of warships Gwydion conjured to frighten Arianrod, or the shape-shifting Merlin practiced to join Uther and Igraine. But the times—and with them the garnering of magic power—had changed since Merlin's day. Even the face of the countryside had changed.

Bacon was born in the west of England, in Somerset, a green and pleasant land quilted with fields where black-faced sheep grazed placidly, and embraced by ranges of rolling hills. In Merlin's time, Somerset, like most of Britain, had been wild country, and many of those hills had been islands, rising from a tremulous sea of fen water. Later generations drained the fens to make rich pastures, thus taming the land to comfortable domesticity.

In Merlin's time, the greatest of the mountainous islands had been Glastonbury Tor, known then as Ynys Avallon—the Isle of Apples—because of the orchards that adorned it. By Bacon's day, the Tor was simply a grassy hill looming 500 feet above the surrounding marshy plain. Curving up the hill's flanks were the stone walls and skyward-reaching towers of an immense and wealthy abbey, where hundreds of monks daily raised their voices in the praising plain song of the Christian Church.

Only a few decades before Bacon's birth, the histories recorded, a remarkable discovery had been made by monks digging in Glastonbury's churchyard. Buried sixteen feet down in a hollowed-out oak bole were the bones of a huge man, and the smaller bones of a woman, along with a tress of her golden hair, "plaited and coiled with consummate skill," according to that indefatigable 12th Century gossip, Gerald of Wales. The skull of the man, he added, had ten wounds in it; the bracelet of bright hair disintegrated to dust when an over-excited young monk leaped into the grave and snatched it up.

The grave had been covered with a stone slab, a lead cross fixed to its underside. "I have seen this cross myself," wrote Gerald, "and I have traced the lettering, which was cut into it on the side turned toward the ground, instead of being on the outer side and immediately visible. The inscription reads as follows: 'Here in the Isle of Avalon lies buried the renowned King Arthur and Guinevere, his second wife.'"

The legends had said of Arthur only that he had sailed after his final battle to the Isle of Avalon—a place undiscovered until the grave was found—and that he still lived there now, waiting for a moment when the British would need him again. It appeared, however, that he had died. Amid speculation about this—and about what wife Arthur might have had besides Guinevere—the abbot of Glastonbury had the bones ceremoniously reinterred.

Almost seven centuries had passed since Merlin and Arthur and all that brave company had disappeared. The world had grown more ordered, a place of bustling cities and busy trade routes that snaked across Europe into Asia and Arabia. As the wilderness receded and commerce extended its reach, the earth became more predictable, more tied to dailiness. The feats of Merlin and his kind were not forgotten, but the new orderliness of the world served as a barrier to the instinctive magic of the elder wizards. Roger Bacon and his fellows had to find other ways to alter the fabric of nature.

As the long years had passed, a civi-

The Provençal prophet

In the days when Europe was plenti-fully supplied with practicing wizards, there lived in France a man named Mi-chel de Nostredame – called Nostrada-mus – whose professions were medi-cine and astrology and whose gift was prophecy. He accurately predicted the deaths of kings, the fall of cities and a host of other great events, al-though the verses in which he cast the prophecies were so cryptic that many were never deciphered.

People said that his prophecies came from observing the stars in their courses, but his power clearly was in-born and not the result of astrological study, as a homely tale tells:

Once, in his physician's capacity, Nostradamus visited a lord whose mother was ailing. As the two men conferred in the castle courtyard, the lord spied a pair of pigs – a black one and a white – and proposed with a smile that the physician should tell the future of the beasts. Nostradamus promptly replied that he and the lord would eat the black one and that a wolf would eat the white.

As a playful trick, the lord secretly ordered that the white pig, not the black, be roasted for supper. That night, as the two men ate, he informed Nostradamus – smacking his lips at the rare taste of his jest – that they were eating white pig. Nostradamus denied it and the cook was summoned to set-tle the argument.

She confessed to her master that they were in fact eating the black pig. She had killed and dressed the white for cooking as ordered, but when she left it unattended in the kitchen, a tame wolf had gnawed it so thorough-ly she was forced to roast the black pig as well, and that was the flesh she had served.

lizing network of cathedrals and monasteries had spread over the countryside. The Church was rich in lands and monies: Throughout fertile Somerset, for instance, the hills were crowned with monastic watchtowers for clerical overseers careful of their acres. And it was rich in learning: While centuries rolled by, while kings rose and fell, while battles were won or lost, while ordinary people followed the changing seasons with plows, seeds and scythes, monks gathered and preserved the wisdom of the ages.

Churchmen were the guardians of the word. In the gray northern light of monastic scriptoria, countless monks patiently copied out the works of Plato and Aristotle and Pythagoras, of Boethius and Avicenna, of their own historians and philosophers. In the same elegant calligraphies found in Roger Bacon's books—with illuminations in gold and important letters in red—the monks defined the architecture of the universe.

The picture was one of wonderful plenitude and majestic logic. Just as human hands had groomed the wild fens of Somerset into a seemly and decorous farm- and pasture-land, human minds had named and fitted everything in creation into a vast and harmonious pattern. The order of things was described in terms of a chain, descending from the base of God's throne, high in the clear empyrean, to the solid earth far below. At the top of the chain were the three orders of angels, beings of pure thought, who—according to some scholars—directed the motions of the heavens, singing as they did so.

Below the angels' starry spheres, all things of the natural world observed degree, priority and place. Nearest the angels was man, the paragon of animals, who possessed the angels' faculty of thought but also summed up in himself all of the earthy phenomena beneath him. Below man came higher animals, such as horses. After these came animate creatures that lacked some senses—oysters, for instance. Then came vegetables, living and growing but immobile and insensate. Lowest of all were inanimate objects, such as stones.

The comforting aspect of this arrangement was that everything fitted and nothing was left out. Everything in nature, no matter how humble, had some special attribute peculiar to itself: A stone, for example, might not be living, but it possessed a durability lacking in a plant, higher on the chain. All the creatures within each class were ranked, too, and every class had a leader: the dolphin among fish, the osprey among birds, the king among men, the seraph among angels, the sun among the heavenly bodies.

But inherent in that cosmic order was great danger, particularly for wizards. No matter what the class, all elements in creation were laced together by mirrored lines and patterns of correspondence. If any part of the delicate balance was disrupted, if any of the strings that made the harmony was untuned, the whole might be affected. Chaos—a real and universal chaos, of dying sun and boiling seas, of famine, plague and fire—could be let loose upon the world.

Indeed, the world was always threatened. To name something is not only to call it into being but also to suggest its opposite: Things are defined in terms of what they are not. Calling into existence an ordered world of light and harmony meant summoning its contrary as well. Hovering at the end of the great chain opposite God was Satan — the Great Adversary — with his hierarchies of demons. He was the implacable enemy of order, the embodiment of discord, destruction and darkness.

Everyone knew the dangers of altering order. Yet being human and informed by human intellect and curiosity — and not averse to the pleasures of power — wizards continued to tamper with the shape of things. They commanded the winds and waves, changed their own forms and those of natural objects, created illusions, summoned up the dead and looked into the future. All of them had some traffic with Satan or with his legions of demons: The Adversary was an ever-interested ally of anyone disposed to alter — and perhaps to damage — the structure of Creation. Some wizards, like Bacon or the Icelandic wizard Sœmundur the Wise or the Scotsman Michael Scot, trod their perilous path warily and ended their lives more or less unscathed. Others, like Bacon's sometime companion Friar Bungay or Wittenberg's vice-ridden Faustus, paid for their power with blood.

Wizards of this era were scholars: Magic now was like a science, its poetry forgotten, and the powers of the wizards came in some part from years of diligent study. The price of living in a finely ordered world was the loss of the intuitive union with nature that the early wizards had possessed. If these later magicmakers were to master nature, they had first to comprehend its patterns and understand the network of correspondences and analogies that bound the universe into a single entity, a macrocosm of which man himself was the miniature reflection.

Central to their studies was their mastery of astrology, the examination of the paths that the planets took through the belt of constellations that girdled the earth (*page* 88). The figures of that great cosmic dance were everywhere mirrored in the world — even in the faces and bodies of humanity — and an understanding of the movements was a very powerful weapon indeed. The progressions of the planets were a map of the future.

The wizards studied terrestrial things, as well, and in particular the four elements — earth, air, fire and water — that they believed were present in varying proportions in all matter. This study found its most ambitious expression in alchemy, which, in the simplest terms, was an investigation of the proportions of the elements in metals, having as its aim the creation of gold. In gold, the king of metals, it was thought that the elements were exactly balanced, as they were in any perfect earthly thing, including the healthy human body. The discovery of that balance would have given a scholar powers far beyond the mere creation of wealth, because it would mean that he would have the key to perfection.

The subject was so profound that it usually was investigated in secrecy, and the cryptic records that survive, replete with mystical symbols, are largely un-

(*continued on page* 70)

Taletelling Cards

ealing in hopes and fears and dreams, scholar-wizards used a pack of richly suggestive cards called the Tarot as a means of telling the future. First a questioner shuffled the deck; then the wizard arranged the cards into formal patterns and meditated on their symbolism (*overleaf*). If skillfully interpreted, the Tarot revealed anything from the success of crops to the movements of distant armies. Most Tarot decks had seventy-eight cards: twenty-two trumps in the Major Arcana and fifty-six face cards and numbered cards in the Minor Arcana. Many readers used the Minor Arcana sparingly or dispensed with it altogether, concentrating instead on the cryptic but powerful trumps — the heart of the Tarot. Each trump had a fine and often baffling plasticity of meaning that let it shift in sense according to its order in the array the wizard dealt, its direction and the vision it inspired in the reader. Vision was the essence of the process: The cards were springboards to intuition, aids to the magician, not substitutes for intuition or magic.

Still, there was a core meaning to each trump — a meaning often closely tied to an allegorical scene shown on its face. The Fool, for example, was usually portrayed as a youth carrying a traveler's staff (*above*). He could represent either initiative or indecision, but he always had to do with fateful choice. And so on for the other cards — the Hermit, the Hanged Man and the rest. Each added its significance to the array and each, in turn, was influenced by the cards it joined.

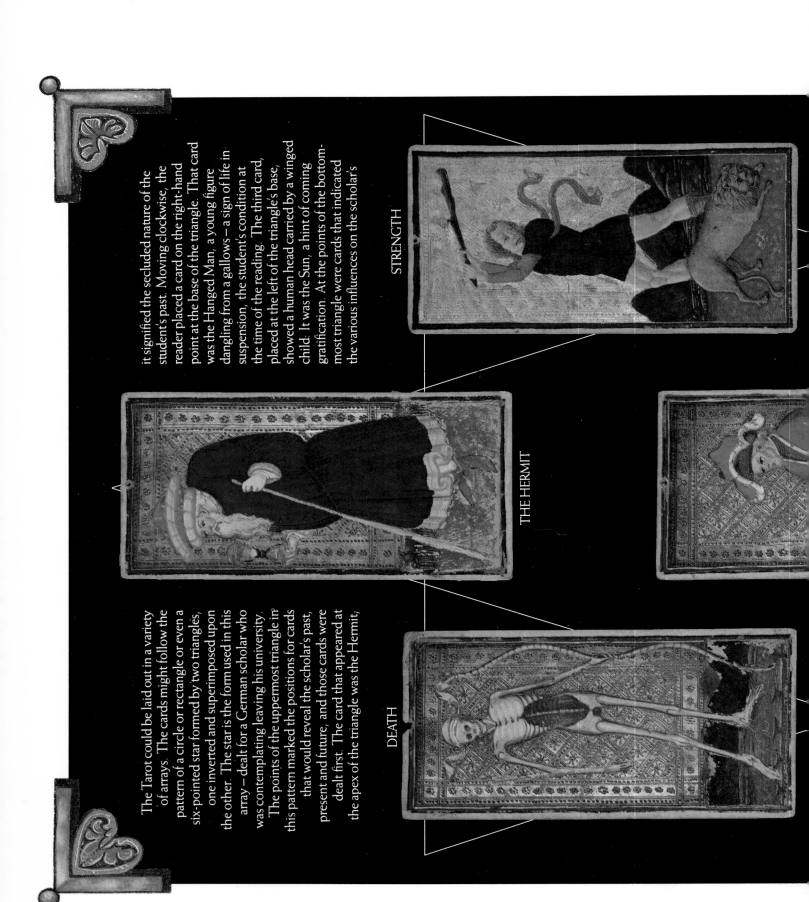

The Tarot could be laid out in a variety of arrays. The cards might follow the pattern of a circle or rectangle or even a six-pointed star formed by two triangles, one inverted and superimposed upon the other. The star is the form used in this array – dealt for a German scholar who was contemplating leaving his university. The points of the uppermost triangle in this pattern marked the positions for cards that would reveal the scholar's past, present and future, and those cards were dealt first. The card that appeared at the apex of the triangle was the Hermit;

it signified the secluded nature of the student's past. Moving clockwise, the reader placed a card on the right-hand point at the base of the triangle. That card was the Hanged Man, a young figure dangling from a gallows – a sign of life in suspension, the student's condition at the time of the reading. The third card, placed at the left of the triangle's base, showed a human head carried by a winged child. It was the Sun, a hint of coming gratification. At the points of the bottom-most triangle were cards that indicated the various influences on the scholar's

STRENGTH

THE HERMIT

DEATH

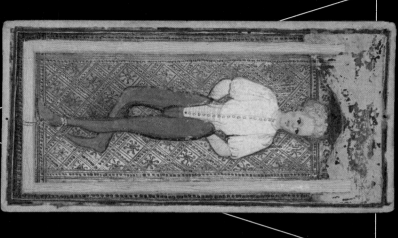

THE HANGED MAN

THE MAGICIAN

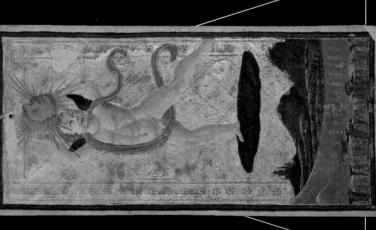

THE WHEEL OF FORTUNE

THE SUN

With the laying of the final card, the scholar's past, present and future all were spread before him. Yet he had to await the reader's interpretation, for the Tarot cards' meaning was veiled behind their gilded decorations. The interpretation given was that because of the strong opposition to the Death card – the card of change – the scholar's life would continue as it had for some time. But change would win out, and the scholar would become a great magician.

And so it happened. The scholar was Doctor Faustus.

future. The first card dealt was ambiguous: On its face blind Fortune stood, but nothing indicated whether she was ally or enemy. The next cards were clearer. Death, a smiling skeleton, indicated that the scholar's life would change; but opposite Death was the card called Strength, indicating opposition to any change. The decisive seventh card was set at the center of the array. It showed the Magician, along with the mysterious symbols of his craft, and what it signified was command over man and nature.

readable. The secrecy helped give rise to wonder-working rumors about all scholars — and not all scholars were wizards. The German sage and alchemist Albertus Magnus, for instance, was credited with the creation of a homunculus, a dwarfish servant with a human shape that walked, thought and obeyed. Unfortunately for itself and its creator, it talked, too — or so the story goes. It prattled incessantly. Nothing could stop it, and the matter of its chatter was ineffably tedious. At last Albertus' pupil Thomas Aquinas became so incensed with the creature that he smashed it into little pieces.

No tale could be more unlikely. Albertus and Thomas were men of towering intellect and irreproachable piety (both were eventually canonized), and neither man would have risked courting the creatures the wizards dealt with.

The schooling of many wizards extended far beyond the conventional arts and sciences of the day. Most of them disappeared for long periods at some point in their careers. When they returned to their own lands, they were haggard, grim-faced and, it was said, accompanied by intermittently visible and long-clawed assistants, who obeyed their every command. People who had dealings with these wizards spoke of a Black School, where magic arts were taught. No one knew quite where it was, but most speculations placed it in Moorish Spain, usually at Toledo or Salamanca.

The sources were agreed about certain details concerning the school. It was in a cavern underground, windowless and lightless, but its books of instruction — whose spells allowed wizards to witness events far away, or to travel great distances in the blink of an eye or to summon up demons — were written in fiery letters that provided their own light for reading. During the term of their schooling — five or seven years — the would-be wizards never ventured outside and never saw their master. All knew who he was, however, for all had been required to make certain agreements with him before entering.

The master was Satan himself, and the scholars agreed that at the end of their schooling, one of each class — the last to the door — would be the devil's prize.

This was obviously playing with eternal fire, although the devil sometimes missed his mark. The Icelandic wizard Sœmundur the Wise, for instance, was the last of his class to leave the cavern, yet he lived to tell the tale because Satan snatched at his shadow instead of at his body. Sœmundur walked solitary afterward, shadowless for the rest of his life. He possessed wizardly power in plenty: It was said of him that he had a demon servant who carried him across the sea at his command and who managed his house and lands. But the devil was merely biding his time, for it also was said that storms of demons swarmed like flies around Sœmundur's deathbed, waiting for his soul to leave his body.

The skills attained at the Black School seemed always to be the same: The scholar Michael Scot, for instance – a wizard almost contemporary with Roger Bacon – returned from Spain in command of innumerable demonic servants and in possession of a tome called *The Book of Might*, which contained the spells to release or restrain them. He is said to have flown on a demon that had taken the shape of a horse, to have summoned rich banquets from out of the air, to have forced his infernal helpers to build bridges and change the shape of mountains.

Yet Michael Scot was frightening to the ordinary people around him. When he died, he was buried with respect and *The Book of Might* was hung on the church wall near his grave; but for centuries afterward, people refused to open the book, or even to touch it, for fear of releasing the creatures its spells commanded.

The reason for their fear, of course, was that Scot was in league with the enemy of the universe, imperiling himself, those near him and the very order of nature. It was no easy matter to touch pitch without being defiled. A wizard had to have great bravery and skill to command and guide the powers of darkness without being absorbed by them.

In this respect, Roger Bacon was a paragon among wizards. Some of the friar's strength, it appears, derived from his charity: He summoned up the tormented

Diviners of the far North

When people talked of wizardry, their thoughts turned to Lapland and Iceland, where the sun shone at midnight and magic was not a secret thing but a commonplace – the "Foible of the North," a traveler called it. Even the Swedes, Northerners themselves, marveled at the practices of their neighbors at the top of the world.

According to the Swedish archbishop Olaf Magnussen, for instance, no Northern king or commoner would risk an enterprise without first examining the future, and their wizards were expert at this. They divined clues in the darting of rabbits and reindeer, the leaping of fish and the flight of birds passing north, then south, each year. They forecast by the stars that fell in the long winter night, by the wind that sang in the mountains and by the smoky exhalations of volcanoes.

But their greatest power was over their icy oceans. Magnussen told of a wizard who charmed a whalebone and rode it across the seas, guiding it by a spell that emanated from his hands. Most wizards, however, were content to control the winds upon which seafaring Northerners depended for commerce and conquest alike. These enterprising magicworkers sold ropes composed of knots of wind to merchants whose ships lay off their stormy coasts. When loosed, the first knot in a rope freed a tranquil and pleasant breeze; the second a boisterous wind; the third, used only at great peril, a veritable tempest.

The Black School

Some brave wizards of Europe, it was said, learned forbidden knowledge in a school presumed to be in Spain – a cavern reached by winding staircases leading far into the earth and sealed from the sunlight by iron doors.

Except for their own murmurings, the scholars had a silent schooling. They saw no schoolmaster and heard no responses to their questions: The answers they asked for each night appeared in the morning as letters that glowed and faded on the pages of their books or shone from the cavern walls. No servants brought the wizards sustenance. Instead, a shaggy hand thrust out from the walls the food and drink they required. No fee was asked save one – that the last man to leave each class give his body and soul to the schoolmaster, whose name was Satan.

ghost of Julian the Apostate—the Fourth Century Roman emperor who had renounced Christianity—to frighten an atheist soldier into right behavior, but he called no diabolical servant for his own selfish ends. Once, it is true, he dealt with Satan himself, but that was an attempt to save a stranger he met on the road.

It happened this way. One day, as Bacon walked the country lanes of Oxfordshire, deep in contemplation, he came upon a young man seated on a grassy knoll, his sword across his knees and tears in his eyes. The friar stopped to give comfort—and to prevent the youth from doing himself an injury, as seemed likely—and thus heard a curious tale.

The young man had been a profligate: Having squandered his inheritance on drink and gambled away his lands, he entered into a contract with an old man who had appeared with an offer of aid. The bargain they struck was that the old man would settle all of the young man's debts and give him the wherewithal to live; in payment, the young man would become the old one's to command. The debts were indeed paid, and the old man had come to claim his due. Only then did the youth realize—by a sudden, sickening whiff of rotting flesh and the sight of glittering eyes in the shadow of the old man's hood—who his creditor was. Because he had been tricked, he was able to argue for a day's grace before the final reckoning, and that day was now ending.

Bacon's face grew grave as he listened. But he offered to help: There was a human soul at stake. He stayed with the youth through the long night, and in the chill dawn of the following morning, they went together to meet Satan at the edge of a wood in the north part of the county.

All seemed peaceful when they arrived at the meeting place. The air was smoky that morning, but this could have been because of charcoal burners at work in the wood. An old man, gowned and hooded in black, awaited them. He looked innocuous enough, although his face was hidden in shadow. When he raised his hand and his sleeve fell back, however, even Bacon flinched. There was no arm attached to the hand.

They got to the business quickly. The old man called on Bacon to witness the contract he held, which did in fact specify that when all the young man's debts were paid, the youth "should be at the lender's disposing, and his without any delay, freely to yield himself upon the first demand of the aforesaid lender."

Bacon read the contract through, then, more thoughtfully, read it once more. Finally he asked the youth, "This is your signature? You agreed that when all your debts were paid, you would give yourself to Satan here?"

"That is so," replied the youth, "but I did not know it was he when I signed."

Bacon waved this aside. He said, "But it is clear to me that all your debts are not yet paid. You have not paid this creditor who stands before us. And as long as that debt remains unpaid, he has no claim." And the friar turned to the old man, his right hand tracing the sign of the cross in the air. But the hooded figure had vanished.

Unlike Bacon, many wizards made a habit of summoning demons. The evi-

(continued on page 79)

Legions of the Night

When people had nothing more than candles to keep out the dark, the hours between dusk and dawn brought forth a seething horde of spirits. They appeared at random, as shapeless shadows or in hastily assumed bodies that were patchworks of stolen parts—goats' hoofs and cats' claws, dogs' fangs and human faces. Aimlessly evil, they huddled in hedgerows or scrabbled at doorways and window shutters, waiting for the chance to pinch and claw, to corrupt and maim and kill. Ordinary people referred to such spirits as bogies, boggarts or goblins, and they regarded them with dread. Scholars and wizards feared the creatures, too, but they sought to master and command the creatures' supernatural strengths, channeling them

Eurynome

to human purposes. The scholar-wizards referred to them as demons, or sometimes as imps. The latter word, which originally referred to tree grafting, had come to mean "offshoot" or "offspring," and when wizards used the term, they meant that the creatures were the offspring of Satan, the Great Adversary.

To define the powers of the demons was a step toward mastery, and the scholars took the activity to amazing extremes. For instance, the most assiduous among them claimed that the assorted spirits that haunted the world formed a hellish hierarchy commanded by Satan and organized in classical fashion into six legions. Each legion had sixty-six cohorts, or military divisions; each cohort had 666 companies and each company had 6,666 soldiers. This army of the night, however, seems excessively fanciful: The total number of demons in the system would have exceeded a billion—a population greater than all the human beings then on earth.

Most scholars were less concerned with such arithmetic than they were with the naming and characterization of particular demonic spirits; these

Xaphan

Ronwe

were the creatures that sorcerers such as Doctor Faustus and
Friar Bungay sought, summoned and controlled with magic circles
and chanted spells.

The characterization of powerful demons was made difficult by
the fact that they were supreme shape shifters. In order to go about
its infernal business in the mortal world, an imp was quite capable of
assuming a commonplace and innocuous shape. It might appear as a
domestic animal such as a dog—as the demon Mephistopheles did
when he was serving Faustus—or as a fly or a toad or a mouse in order
to go about its work unnoticed.

Its real shape, usually seen only by those scholar-wizards brave
enough to summon it by name, was a hideous reflection of its
essentially malevolent nature, a twisted mockery of the living forms

of the natural
world. There was
Eurynome, for
instance. Ghoul-
ishly wrinkled, sharp-
toothed, and clawed
hand and foot, Eurynome
was an eater of carrion. He was
said to be Satan's Prince of
Death, and his services, if they
could be commanded, were useful
for the murderously inclined. A
demon named Ronwe—squat,
coarse, big-eared and betailed—
could grant the understanding of
all languages, a formidable weapon
for spellworkers. Xaphan, with his
ever-present bellows, was simply an
ugly curiosity; he occupied himself, it was said, by fanning the
eternal flames of hell. Orobas
ranked high in the infernal re-

Orobas

gions. When summoned, he appeared sometimes as a man and sometimes as a horse, and he could tell the summoner the truths about all the happenings of history or predict the course of events in times to come. Astaroth, called the Grand Duke of Hell, appeared on some occasions as a parti-colored man and on others as the fallen angel that he was, his once-beautiful angel's face distorted, his splendid wings dulled. He brought with him, it is said, a stench so terrible that wizards summoning him carried a silver ring, supposed to be protection against the demonic miasma. Like Orobas, Astaroth could reveal the lost past and predict the future, and he knew the full meaning of any of the arts of man or sorcerer.

Wizards could summon many other Satanic servants — Abracax and Flauros, Behemoth and Belial, Buer and Asmodeus — and their powers were carefully recorded. The rewards of enlisting their aid could be great, of course. But wizards often found, as Faustus did when he made his pact with Mephistopheles, that the price was very high indeed.

Astaroth

dence appears in the multitude of formulas for conjuration found in the *grimoires,* books of magical instruction. (*The Key of Solomon* was the most famous.)

The formulas derived from diverse ancient sources and therefore varied considerably in detail, but the general patterns of activity were the same. To summon a demon, the conjurer drew a circle — usually nine feet in diameter — around himself. The circle might be drawn on the floor with charcoal or on the ground with a sword or with a ceremonial knife called an *arthame;* it might enclose smaller circles or pentacles, five-pointed stars; it might be inscribed with Hebrew and Greek characters signifying the different names of God or other protective words.

The most important requirement was that the circle be unbroken. It thus became a powerful symbol of eternity, because it had no beginning and no end. It was a whole, a mirror of the universe. In the space within the circle, the wizard's inspiration was mightily concentrated; the line that formed the circle became a defensive barrier against the inimical creatures he conjured. As long as the wizard remained within the line, he was safe to begin speaking the words that called the creatures of Satan. Some magic books gave words from unknown languages: One formula began, "*Bagabi laca bachabe / Lamac cahi achababe,*" and continued with these curious syllables for nine lines. In other cases, the demons were summoned in the name of God himself, and wizards called upon them to come "visibly and without delay, in a fair human form, not terrifying." Every effort toward self-protection was made, and the

most important not forgotten: The wizard must stay within his circle; if he put so much as a finger outside, he was doomed.

Although wizards sometimes conjured up Satan's minions to perform particular tasks, the most common motive was to enter into a diabolical contract — the same grim bargain that Bacon's young companion unwittingly agreed to. Perhaps the earliest recorded such contract was that of a Sixth Century cleric named Theophilus, who sold his soul just to obtain church office. The practice was well known enough that even popes were accused of trading their souls for papal crowns.

A wizard could get much more than high office, however. In exchange for his soul, he could gain mastery over nature for the remainder of his life. By deliberately committing himself to the powers of evil — abjuring all that was good in the order of the universe, from the smallest growing flower to the stars and planets in their stately dance — he ensured the fulfillment of his every wish and whim. The Prince of Darkness was a gentleman and always kept his word. And having all eternity, Satan could afford to wait for the inevitable close of one small life, when the promised soul became his to devour.

But absolute power corrupts absolutely, and the wizards who made the contracts seemed to live joyless and frantic lives, always shadowed by the horror that lay waiting at the end. Nowhere is this so evident as in the history of Doctor Faustus, a wizard who lived some years after Bacon and in a different country. Centuries after his death, he was made into a kind of hero, but the early Faustus legends tell a different tale.

The story begins in Germany, at Wittenberg, an ancient university town on the Elbe River. There in his youth went John Faustus, sent by his parents to study divinity. He distinguished himself in the years he was a scholar. His performance was so brilliant, in fact, that the university rectors and masters—"with one consent," the tale says—made him a Doctor of Divinity. The irony they could not appreciate was that, from the very beginning, the divinity scholar had also privately studied the arts of conjuration and necromancy—the raising of the dead for the purposes of inquiring about the afterlife. His strong and nervous intellect found its clerical diet insipid.

In the decades that followed, the acquisition of magical power became an obsession for Faustus. He renounced the divinity degree, to the relief of other scholars. As evidenced by his miserably deteriorating body—white beard, raddled skin, shaking hands—his life was a debauch, a never-ending round of drinking and whoring. Inevitably, he developed a craving for sensations beyond what Wittenberg could provide.

One night Faustus left behind the narrow winding streets and steeply gabled roofs of the town and walked alone to a thick wood in the country. He came to a crossroads (the power of in-between places was not forgotten), and there in the dust he drew a circle. Standing within it, he drew more circles and also certain characters. Just before nine o'clock he began to chant, calling an underworld prince whose name was Mephistopheles. He paused, and in the distance heard the bells of the town echoing coldly from hill to hill as they announced the hour. A wind rose suddenly in the wood, so strong that it bent the tree trunks and roared among the branches. Faustus heard a drum-roll of thunder and saw bright stabs of lightning. But no rain fell, and the sounds died away.

He chanted again.

A dragon flashed fiery coils among the stars, and a hoarse voice suddenly spoke Faustus' name. From the shadows of the trees came a rending howl, as if the trees themselves were keening. Then a globe of fire—a will-o'-the-wisp the size of a man—appeared at the very rim of the circle drawn in the dust.

Faustus cried "Mephistopheles!" The fiery globe split and trembled and dimmed and disappeared. In its place stood a mild-looking, middle-aged man dressed in a friar's habit.

"Will you step outside your circle, Faustus?" said the friar, pronouncing the words with an unpleasant hiss.

Faustus refused. There was a resigned sigh, and the friar asked, "Then what is your request?"

"That, leaving me unharmed, you come to me at midnight in the privacy of my chambers. I wish to make a pact with you."

"I am bound to do so," the friar replied, and Faustus found himself alone again.

He returned to the sleeping town and walked through empty streets to his own rooms to await Mephistopheles. The wait was a short one, but for Faustus it was full of shiverings: Something about his chambers seemed not quite right. He had the impression that eyes watched him from inside the walls; he turned to look and saw only the walls. When he sat at his desk he thought he heard rustlings and scrabblings — and worst of all, the click of teeth — near the entrance to the room. But when he glanced in that direction he saw only an empty archway. The minutes of waiting were a foretaste of the future. Faustus was never to be alone again.

Mephistopheles appeared without warning at the stroke of midnight, but not as a friar. He was as gaudily bedecked as a court jester and bejeweled as a sultan. He drifted restlessly around the room while he and Faustus talked. They could not come to an agreement: Faustus wanted to have the services of the demon without having to surrender his own soul, even though Mephistopheles pointed out that his master would never permit it.

In the end, they met twice more before Faustus took up his quill. "Now have I, Doctor John Faustus, unto the hellish prince and his messenger Mephistopheles given both body and soul," he wrote, "upon such condition that they shall teach me and fulfill my desire in all things." His term was to be twenty-four years, he continued, and he ended the statement with a string of blasphemies. The contract was written and signed in Faustus' own blood.

"Now my pleasures begin," he said when he had finished.

"Yes, indeed, my Faustus," said Mephistopheles in tranquil tones.

Faustus now had the ultimate powers a wizard could possess, and he might have done great deeds. But the record of his twenty-four years was one of drunkenness and buffoonery, of lies and lechery.

There could be no doubting the strength of his supernatural aid. His appearance altered amazingly for the better. (This, he said, was because Mephistopheles had taken him to the den of a sorceress. The woman — who was assisted by an assortment of talking cats and apes — gave him a fiery potion that made him young again.) He was companioned by the most beautiful woman in the world. And he was served by a large black spaniel that possessed quite un-doglike powers: When Faustus told the beast to produce food or drink or women for his friends, the orders were instantly obeyed. The spaniel, he later said — with lascivious detail — once allowed him to observe a Beltane Eve witches' orgy in the Harz Mountains.

For the most part, Faustus contrived at petty and nasty tricks. When a priest refused him drink, he devised a vengeful gift, a lotion that removed hair and saved the necessity of shaving — but that (as the priest found out too late) took off skin as well. He caused a cuckold's horns to grow on the brow of a harmless knight in Innsbruck, and when the knight chased him over the fields outside the city, he caused the bushes of the countryside to change into mounted musketeers, who brought the knight to his knees. Annoyed by the antics of a group of students he caroused with, he had Mephistopheles create the illusion that they were in a vineyard; in snatching at the wine jugs, they unwittingly beat one another bloody and senseless.

It was a sorry performance, and its final act contemptible. A month before the contract came due, Faustus dismissed Mephistopheles and turned to loud lamentation and repentance. He prayed. He read the gospel. He lectured his drinking companions – the few that were left – on the dangers of vice. And he kept them close beside him; Faustus had no taste for solitude.

On the eve of his day of reckoning, Faustus left his own house in Wittenberg and repaired to an inn in the village of Rimlich, accompanied by his friends, who later said that they had spent the evening drinking while Faustus wept for his sins. One of them said he had seen a large black spaniel crouching at the inn door; thinking it to be Faustus' dog, he opened the door for it, but the animal refused to enter.

Eventually the company went to bed, leaving Faustus alone. All agreed later that the inn was quiet, so quiet that they heard the bells of Wittenberg strike midnight.

A wind rose up then, they said. It blew steadily, beating branches against the windows and rattling doors on their hinges. They heard a ground-floor door slam. The wind hissed up the stairs and into the passageway outside their chambers. Each man saw his own door tremble and strain at its hinges, then heard the creak of his neighbor's as the wind passed by. Last of all they heard a crash at the door that barred the room where Faustus lay.

A gurgling scream echoed down the passageway, and then another, a fearsome howling that brought the guests bolt upright in their beds. One man thought of a fox in the snare, another of the rack and thumbscrews. Then there was nothing.

The wind died suddenly. The rest of the night was profoundly peaceful.

But none of the company slept and none left his room. When the dawn came, they gathered in the passageway and together went to Faustus' chamber. The first man in blanched and turned away. The chamber was a charnel house. Swaths of blood were painted on the walls and spattered on the ceiling. A gray mass adhered limply to one wall – the contents of Faustus' smashed skull. In a corner, a disembodied eye stared upward from the floor.

The rest of the body – bitten, clawed and cruelly distorted – was found in the stableyard below the room, flung across a pile of horse dung.

For decades after that – until it was torn down, in fact – no one would live in Faustus' house in Wittenberg. It was too dark and cold and still, and those who passed by at night said that they had seen a pallid, one-eyed face staring at them from an upper window.

Faustus' death was the most lurid of its kind, but there had been others. One of these, years before, had touched Roger Bacon himself and influenced the curious choice he made at the end of his long life.

Bacon sometimes traveled with a companion called Friar Bungay, a cheerful roisterer and a wizard of a rather minor sort. Bungay maintained a running feud with a sorcerer named Vandermast, which for years involved activities no more irritating than duels of spirit-raising and dunkings in streams. Finally, however, Bungay played an especially humiliating

Once summoned by old Faustus the wizard, the demon Mephistopheles had only
to smile his secret smile and wait until the mortal sold his soul for pleasure.
Then Faustus became a player and Mephistopheles the master of the show. . . .

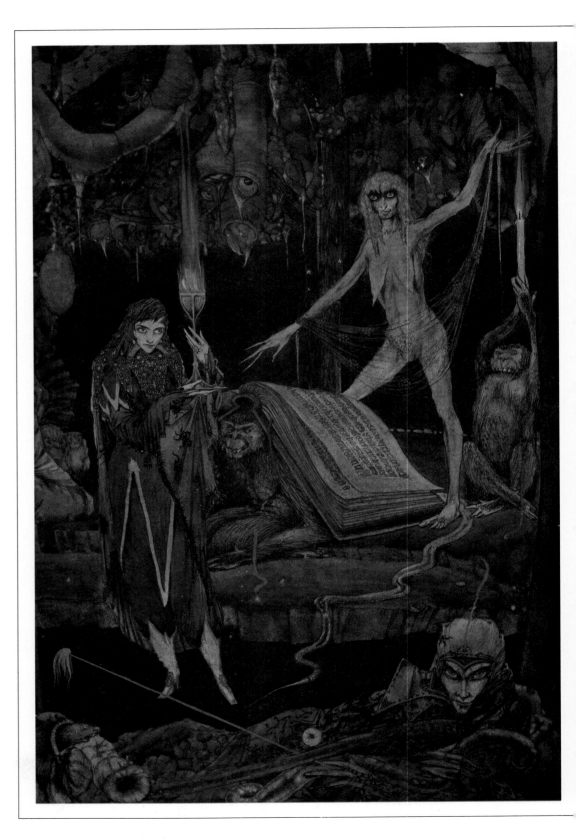

The setting for the first act of Faustus' new career was the cavern of a
witch, who pleased the old man's vanity with an elixir of youth. As
Mephistopheles looked on, the years fell from the wizard while foul apes sniggered.

The second act took place in a tavern, where Faustus took pleasure in pain.
Mephistopheles made healthy young men fight like beasts, while safe in a
corner Faustus watched the blood spurt. Close by his shoulder, the demon smiled. . . .

Mephistopheles' third act gratified Faustus' lust: On a high mountain peak, the demon showed the wizard the trances of a witches' dance. While Faustus leered, his demon mused happily upon his own reward.

trick on Vandermast: He caused the sorcerer to be spirited into a pond while the man was making love. After that, matters escalated, until the pair, alone together in the dead of night, apparently tried a battle with demons. They were found the next morning, charred and lifeless, near the scorched remains of two magic circles.

At about this time, two young students went to Bacon's chambers at Oxford with a simple request: They wanted to see how their fathers were. Bacon had a magic looking glass — probably made of beryl, the stone most commonly used for the purpose — that enabled him to see events occurring as many as fifty miles away. He knew both the fathers and the sons, and being of a generous nature, he granted the students' request.

Bacon withdrew the glass from its hiding place and held it up for the boys. They named their fathers. The surface of the glass, blue and misty at first, gradually cleared to reveal the figures of two old men, tiny and distant, but clearly the fathers of the boys. The boys watched transfixed as the silent actors — once fast friends — shook their fists at each other. Then one of the figures drew his sword without ceremony and hacked the other down. Bacon covered the glass quickly and began to speak, but the damage had been done. One son demanded revenge; the other defended his parent, although neither could tell what had caused the fatal battle. In an instant daggers were drawn, and in another the two boys lay mortally wounded on the floor of Bacon's study.

After this, Bacon altered. He retired to his chamber and allowed admittance to no one, save for the messenger who delivered the news about Friar Bungay. Days later, he emerged gaunt and pale. He had resolved to abjure his magic. It was knowledge, he said, not meant for fallible mortals, and too much death attended the practice. Its burden had become too heavy for him to bear.

Bacon himself cleared his university chambers of their decades of clutter. Useful objects — his prisms and mirrors, his lovingly assembled bird skeletons, his astronomical equipment — he gave away to the more lean and threadbare of his students. But the magic books were burned. Bacon built a bonfire for his *Key of Solomon* and his Arabic *Picatrix*, his Persian *Canon* and other studies. Cast onto the flames, the gilded pages curled and blackened, the gold ran like tears, the painted diagrams peeled and crackled, and the letters soared off as smoke. "In that flame," says one account sadly, "burnt the greatest learning in the world."

At last, shorn of his enchantments, the aged friar retired to an anchorite's cell built into the wall of a church. Two years after that, he died and his fellow friars laid him in his grave.

Bacon was not, of course, the last worker of magic. Other wizards followed him, and witches, too, the wizards' humble cousins. But among the watchers of the universe who dared to alter its order, the kindest and the best was Roger Bacon. It is fitting that affectionate memories cherished tales of his prowess for centuries, long after he had gone to dust.

Tidings of the Heavens

In earlier times, the heavens seemed charged with meaning, and astrologer-wizards gazed into the star-fretted night to seek, in the orderly procession of the heavenly bodies, intelligence about what was past or passing or to come. The scholars defined the universe — whose overarching structure was everywhere reflected in the world and in humankind — in terms of a band of constellations, a belt around the world that formed the twelve signs of the zodiac. Traveling through this slowly wheeling net of stars, the Sun, the Moon and the five planets nearest the Earth pursued their own majestic courses, guardians and rulers of the constellations they crossed. Stargazers studied the relative positions of the bodies in this cosmic dance, searching for the correspondences that gave insight into the patterns of earthly life.

courge of winter and source of light and life, the Sun was the biggest and most influential of celestial bodies, the glorious lamp of heaven and its king. Appropriately, the Sun ruled that part of the sky marked by the constellation Leo, a regal exemplar of dignity, magnanimity and creativity. But all the planets and constellations came under the rule of the Sun, for its yearly path — called the ecliptic — passed exactly through the center of the zodiacal belt. The life of the Earth came from the Sun, as well as human strength and health, which was why the Sun was depicted as shining down on sporting exercises.

After the Sun came the Moon, queen to the Sun's king, a female principle to answer the male — responsive, instinctual and so sensitive and sympathetic that it seemed almost to dissolve into whatever it touched.

The Moon held sway over the constellation Cancer, the Crab — an appropriately changeable water sign — but like the Sun, the Moon brought any sign it occupied into prominence. It was associated with all things of feeling, with giving birth and with motherhood, home and family. Above all, however, the Moon was the mistress of flux, tugging rhythmically at the tides of the oceans and those of human feeling alike.

91

Each planet controlled two constellations, or signs of the zodiac. Warlike Mars ruled over Aries the Ram and Scorpio the Scorpion, sharing the beast's courage and the insect's stinging intensity. Mars governed battles and all who fought them.

Wing-footed Mercury, the fastest of the planets, had an altogether more peaceful reign, dominating the witty and versatile Gemini, or Twins, and the modest, diligent Virgo – the Virgin. Mercury had powers over travel, the arts, commerce and agriculture.

Disasters and violent death flowed from Saturn, outermost of the five planets. Saturn stood for limitation, contraction and loss. The determined Goat, Capricorn, and eccentric Aquarius the Waterbearer were under Saturn's rule, which tended toward disorder and chaos. Huge Jupiter was Saturn's opposite. Expansive, optimistic, protective, fatherly, the planet controlled Pisces the Fish and the Archer, Sagittarius, symbols respectively of tolerance and justice.

Venus ruled Libra the Scales and the persistent, possessive Bull of Taurus. Venus was a force for harmony, unison and fruitfulness; the planet's influence brought men and women together, in love, in dance and in society generally.

s the planets governed the zodiac, so the zodiac governed the human body, that microcosm of all creation. Each sign of a constellation dominated one organ or part of the body. Appropriately enough, the butting Ram had power over the head, the Bull had power over the neck and shoulders, and the Twins, Fish and Scales – three pairs – over the arms, feet and kidneys. The Lion ruled the heart. The shieldlike Crab controlled the chest, the Virgin the belly and the Scorpion the sexual organs, while the legs were governed by the Archer, the Goat and the Waterbearer.

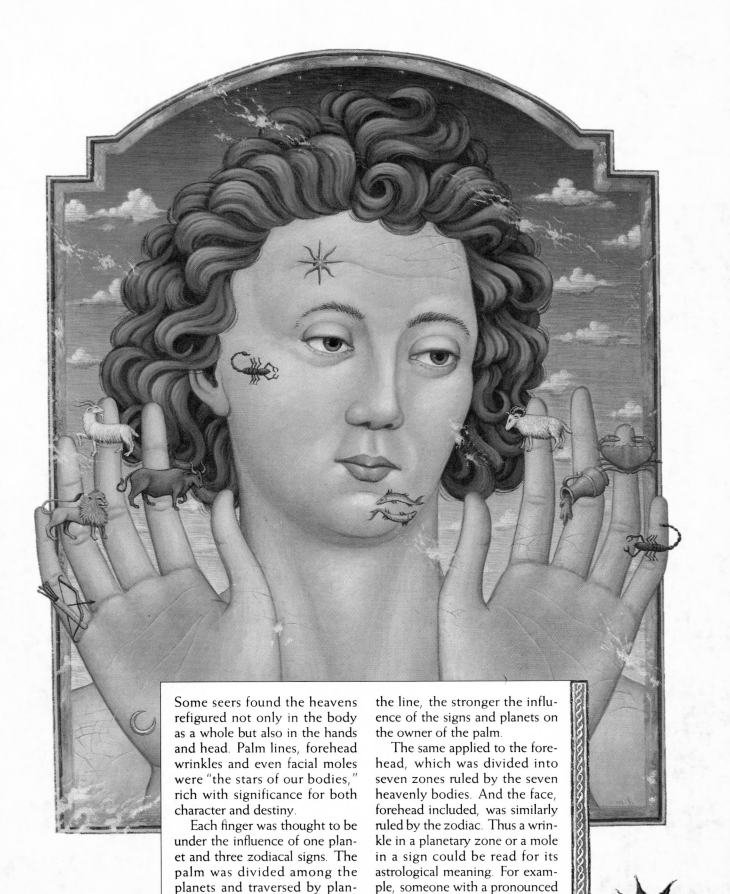

Some seers found the heavens refigured not only in the body as a whole but also in the hands and head. Palm lines, forehead wrinkles and even facial moles were "the stars of our bodies," rich with significance for both character and destiny.

Each finger was thought to be under the influence of one planet and three zodiacal signs. The palm was divided among the planets and traversed by planetary lines governing luck, intuition and health. The longer, straighter and more continuous the line, the stronger the influence of the signs and planets on the owner of the palm.

The same applied to the forehead, which was divided into seven zones ruled by the seven heavenly bodies. And the face, forehead included, was similarly ruled by the zodiac. Thus a wrinkle in a planetary zone or a mole in a sign could be read for its astrological meaning. For example, someone with a pronounced wrinkle in the area governed by the Sun would be likely to acquire great power.

Ordinary folk huddled fearfully in their beds when, with a rush of wind and a skirl of laughter, witches coursed the nighttime sky.

Chapter Three

The Shadowy Sisterhood

One frosty autumn morning many centuries past, a curious little drama unfolded against the placid setting of an English farming village. At the edge of this village was a close — a small, hedged-in area of land where a farmer stabled his four milk cows at night. Beside the close, crouched in the shadow of the hedge, was the farmer himself, holding his scythe across his knees. He waited stolidly in this position, as he had waited all the long night through, while good folk in his village slept safe in their beds. All good folk but one, that is. That one — not yet identified — was a thief, who each night stole the milk from the farmer's cows and left the animals torn and injured.

The morning star faded, the moon grew pale and slipped from sight, the cows slept on, and the farmer watched. Nothing stirred. Then a hare, silky-furred, silver-gray and almost invisible in the faint light, hopped from the shadows into the close. As soon as it touched the open ground, it sat up on its haunches and froze—eyes shining, long ears erect, motionless except for twitching nostrils and whiskers. The farmer, downwind of the hare and therefore unnoticed, watched but made no move. It was a pretty little creature, after all, and as long as it kept clear of his vegetable patch, he was prepared to let it go about its business.

But what was this hare's business? Satisfied of safety, it dropped to all fours and hopped unconcernedly among the hoofs of the cattle, where it reared again, showing its long shining teeth as it reached greedily toward an udder.

After a horrified moment, the farmer sprang like an avenging angel from his hiding place, lifting his scythe. He brought down the blade in a murderous arc as the terrified hare streaked past him. At first, he thought he had missed the mark, but then the animal gave a savage shriek. The hare vanished through the hedge. On the ground of the close lay its forepaw, severed at the first joint.

The farmer set down his scythe and calmed his frightened cattle, brushing them down with a handful of straw while he thought about the matter. By the time he had finished his work, the cocks had begun to crow and the morning light to glow in crimson streaks in the east. He picked up the hare's foot, wrapped it carefully in a rag and, balancing his scythe upon his shoulder, set off down the dusty lane that led through his village.

A trail of blood in the dust made it clear that the hare had fled not to the safety of the rye and barley fields surrounding the village, but into the village. The farmer followed this dismal track past the gardens and cottages of his waking neighbors, past the churchyard with its brooding yew trees, past the village well. At the well, the tiny stains, now browning in the dust, led down another lane to a house the farmer knew—as he did every house in his village.

The hare had gone to ground, it seemed, at the very doorstep of a goodwife of that neighborhood, the widow of a freeman like himself. The farmer stood in her small yard and looked around, but everything seemed as usual. The house thatch steamed as the morning sun thawed its mantle of frost; woodsmoke drifted fragrantly from the eaves, showing that the goodwife was up and about her work. In the yard, three beehives stood in a row on their bench, the colonies quiet; ducks and geese pecked in the dirt around the farmer's feet. The wounded hare was nowhere to be seen.

Leaning his scythe against the cottage wall, the farmer stepped through the door of the cottage and called his neighbor's name. There was no answer, but as far as he could see in the dim light, all was in order. Everywhere were the signs of the thrifty housewife: in the sweet-smelling bunches of herbs drying on the wall, in the massive hams hanging from the ridgepole to cure in the woodsmoke, in neatly stacked sacks of grain, in baskets of carded wool, in distaff and spindle, in the butter churn and cheese molds. The little cottage was much like his own.

The housewife herself he saw last, after his eyes grew accustomed to the shadows.

She was crouched in a far corner, her back to him. She gave forth a stream of whimpering mumbles, horrible to hear.

"Goodwife," began the farmer gently.

The woman swung around to confront him. Her face was ashen, and at her bosom she clutched a scarlet bundle. She bared her teeth, gibbering at the farmer, and stretched the arm that held the bundle toward him. The bandages fell away to reveal the bloody stump of the woman's right arm, severed at the wrist joint. The farmer took a step backward and shifted his glance away from the sunken, glittering eyes. His hand came up in the sign that turned evil aside.

"You are a witch, then," said he, and began to edge toward the door.

"Give back the hare's foot," said she.

"Oh no," said he, "I'll keep it for luck." And he fled to the safety of the lane.

That such a thing could be so was no cause for wonderment: Country people had known of witches and their ways for time out of mind. The woman had simply changed her shape to that of an animal and, when wounded as an animal, carried the wound when she reverted to her human form. In her animal shape she had engaged in one form of malevolence commonplace among witches—stealing the milk that nourished people's bodies.

But talk of witches can be no more simple and straightforward than witchcraft itself. Little about these matters was written down, and that little is often confusing and contradictory—fragmentary tales and observations of anonymous people in unnamed villages. In later centuries, there were, of course, the records of the

Workaday witchery

Wherever there were witches, there were whispers — rumors and suspicions of malevolent handiwork in many forms. A farmer whose cow was going dry, for instance, was advised to look for signs of theft by an evil neighbor. One such sign was a milk-spattered ax handle, for witches were known to charm cows' milk into axes, sparing themselves the necessity of approaching the cows.

Then there was weatherworking — the management of wind and rain. It was done in all sorts of ways, the gossips said. For instance, a witch might simply brew up a storm in a caldron, a process much like that of making a gargantuan stew.

All of this was rather elementary magic compared with the darker deeds that villagers imagined. Having heard of the complex rites and learned incantations that wizards used to summon demons, country folk assumed that witches, too, used magic circles and spells in arcane languages to call up uncanny aid. They might have been correct, but it was unlikely that more than a few witches pursued this sophisticated practice: Most witches were unlettered villagers themselves, not scholars like the wizards.

A soft-footed servant

In ways both physical and behavioral, the hare was a natural ally of witches: Hares are swift and agile, able to stand on their hind legs like a person, prone to gathering in parliament-like groups, orgiastically mad in the spring, wantonly destructive of crops and possessed of a most unbeastlike cry. Some witches traveled in the shape of hares; others had hare familiars – demonic servants in disguise.

Given the association of hares with witchcraft and magic, it is not surprising that superstition surrounded them. It was said, for example, that the sight of a hare running down a village street presaged fire and that the appearance of a white hare in a mine would be followed by a fatal accident. A hare who crossed a person's path would bring bad luck. And the very word "hare" could not be mentioned at sea, so great was the fear of the animal's power.

Curiously enough, possession of a hare's-foot brought luck. This belief arose not from the hare's traffic with witches but from much more ancient associations: The hare is a notably prolific creature, and its foot was long a sexual symbol.

Church's Inquisition, but the transcripts of witchcraft trials – piteous records of the torture and murder of thousands of innocent people – reveal only superstition and outright invention. The trial records gauge the Church's determination to thwart deviation from its norms, but they rarely cast light on real witches. Their story must be teased from the scanty evidence of earlier times, before the trials.

In those days, while Roger Bacon and his fellows conversed with kings or practiced their sophisticated sorceries in the universities and in royal courts, the mass of humankind followed the rhythmic cycle of the farmer's seasons. Almost everyone lived in small villages nestled among long furrowed fields and broad patches of forest. People's lives revolved around those of their near neighbors, for the villages were isolated: One might be three hours' walk from the next, or a day or two days, and the walk would lead along rutted tracks that turned into a quagmire as soon as rain began to fall.

So people kept close to their own cottages and fields, their own village wells, their own miller's white-sailed mills and their own blacksmith's smoking forges. They measured out the year in the tasks of sustenance. In the spring they sowed beans, oats and barley and tended the lambing and calving; in summer they sheared their sheep; in the autumn they harvested, planted more crops and slaughtered the animals they could not feed through the cold season. They measured their days in similar fashion – in morning and evening milking and egg gathering; in the weeding of gardens and the threshing and winnowing of grains; in the churning of butter and the making of cheese; in the spinning and weaving of wool; in the getting and bearing of children.

Theirs was a hard life and an uncertain one: In those centuries, famine and plague often stalked the land, and Death on his pale horse was never very far away. Life hung by the slenderest of threads: The failure of a crop or the drying-up of a cow could spell starvation; a wasting disease could turn a hale and hearty man into a trembling skeleton in a matter of weeks.

No one could tell when disaster might strike, for concealed among the country people themselves were the black witches, the age-old enemies of healthy growth and life. Some were descendants of the hags and night riders of time immemorial, evil creatures whose powers apparently were inborn. Others were people who sold their souls to Satan – in the manner of their more distinguished counterparts, the wizards – in exchange for magic power. They could wither crops or steal the goodness – what the English called the *foyson* – from grain, command destructive winds and rains, steal milk or make it sour, or keep rich cream from being churned to butter. They could make men impotent and women miscarry; by the power of a glance alone, they could cause crippling strokes. They were the enemies and, it was said, the devourers of children, who were the living proof of the continuity of life.

The black witch's destructive activities were the same everywhere and in every era: The witches of medieval Europe practiced the same cold magic as those of classical Rome, and they worked by the same methods. It is no wonder that the sign to avert the witch's evil power was the ancient, potent phallic gesture – the arm outstretched, the hand with its two inner fingers curled and its two outer ones stiffly extended.

Other protection – and protectors, as well – existed to ward off the powers of black witchcraft. People could and did hedge themselves with rituals, spells and charms drawn from a body of magic lore and knowledge that had been preserved from generation to generation by good and careful people known variously as "cunning folk," "white witches" or "fairy doctors." These people were healers, skilled by birth (the powers seemed to run in families) and by training in the use of herbs and in midwifery, as well as in weather prediction, in the discovery of theft and sometimes in fortunetelling. White witches seemed to sense when black witchcraft was at work and sometimes could defeat it. And they taught the weaker folk around them how to preserve their health and happiness.

The first rule was to lead a righteous life, adhering to the patterns that helped define the order of the world. Unlettered farmers could not be expected to understand the complex patterns of the cosmos, of course, but they could conduct their affairs according to practical guidelines that sprang from those patterns.

Thus, for instance, lambs should be conceived on September 29, at Michaelmas, the Feast of Saint Michael the Archangel; they should be born at Candlemas, on February 2; and they should be weaned on May 1, the Feast of Saint Philip and Saint James. Beans and garlic should be sowed on the feast day of Saint Edmund the King, November 20. It was unlucky to do any business on December 28, the anniversary of the massacre of the Holy Innocents. And it was unwise to plow on Friday, that being the day of the Crucifixion; stones might be picked from the field then, but the earth could not be disturbed.

All of these rules — and there were similar regulations for every activity — helped preserve the general order and thus buttress the world against agents of disorder.

But also in common use were important protections against witchcraft. One was salt. A preservative of food and a source of health, salt derived its power from its incorruptibility. It was placed in the cradles of newborn babies until they could be baptized; farmers poured it into holes drilled in their plows, hoping to ensure fertile fields; fishermen sprinkled it on their nets for safety at sea. Another protection was strong iron in the form of a horseshoe — symbol of that potent worker of iron, the smith. The horseshoe was hung, horns up, over doorways and on ships' masts. Still other weapons were two herbs that flowered at midsummer: Vervain and St.-John's-wort, hung in houses or carried by travelers, served, it was thought, as barriers against evil.

Of spoken charms against evil there were many, and chief among them were protective spells to be said when night fell, good things of day retreated into sleep, and witches and other dangerous creatures walked freely abroad. Some of these charms, such as the well-known White Paternoster — "Matthew, Mark, Luke and John, bless the bed that I lie on" — were indistinguishable from prayers.

Other charms invoked the powers of goodness to aid the charm-sayer in more specifically aggressive ways. Among the many examples is a night spell intended to protect the beasts of the field. In order to make the spell, the farmer stood in his pasture and invoked Christ on the Cross, adding, "Through the virtue of His might, let no thief enter in this night." These words were followed by a chilling curse, made in the names of the Trinity, on those who dared to tread where the farmer stood. Trespassers would be rooted to the spot, "their lives mightless and their eyes sightless, enclosed about with dread and doubt."

Such common spells and many more were stored in the memories of the cunning folk, for spoken charms — dim memories of the great words of the very first wizards — gave power to the rustic arts these good people practiced. Healing required an understanding of the use of herbs. The white witches could prescribe lemon balm for weak stomachs, periwinkle for treatment of the skin, betony as an aid against insomnia and a preventative of nightmare, lavender for cough. But with each herb went an age-old charm. Thus the power of creeping cinquefoil, chosen for toothache, was made effective by a homely charm, recited for centuries, that began, "Saint Peter was sitting on a marble stone," and ended, "Whoever keeps these words for my sake shall never have the toothache."

Memory, faith and strong character supported the wise white witches. As a rule, they were unimportant country peasants compared with such learned wizards as Roger Bacon and his colleagues, but the very best of them were brave indeed, and quite prepared to battle sickness and evil and creatures of the night, too, as a Welsh tale shows.

The tale begins with a cottage that was infested by a demon or a ghost (its nature was not quite clear from the garbled accounts of those who had had the misfortune to see it). It was certainly evil, and so viciously frightening that not one soul would sleep in the cottage and no one who lived in that village would even approach the building. Eventually an old wise woman – not distinguished, but known for her skill and courage – was told of the creature. She offered to send it about its business by battling it in the night.

Accordingly, she went at dusk to the deserted cottage, taking only her missal and a candle for light. She locked herself in and sat down to read. The last of the daylight died, the moon rose and began its passage across the skies outside, and the hours passed slowly by. No sound disturbed the reader but the rustle of her turning pages, the occasional crackle of her candle flame and the busy scratching scamper of the mice in the walls.

She came to the end of her reading and looked up from the page of her missal. Standing before her in a patch of moonlight was a shapeless mass of shadows, at the top of which glittered two eyes of flickering flame, full of hate and death and decay. The old woman regarded the creature without flinching, and it regarded her.

She would not drop her eyes, and at last it made its challenge. "Thy faith is in that candle flame," it said.

"Demon, thou liest," she replied, and defiantly put out the light. Then she straightened her back, fixed her wise old eyes on the evil points of flame in the darkness before her and prepared to wait out the night.

But the servant of evil – whatever it was – could not match her steadfast and faithful will. The flame points flickered and died. The shadows dissolved in the air and the old woman was left alone in a dark but innocently empty chamber. In the morning she left the little building and went briskly about her chores. No spirit invaded that cottage again.

The rustic skills and courage of wise old women were all very well, as far as they went, but to battle an enemy, one had first to know who the enemy was. That was the dilemma in dealing with evil witches: They were extraordinarily elusive. They lived – disguised as perfectly ordinary folk – in

Golden maid in a stony cage

When German villagers whiled away the winter nights with talk of witches, they told this tale: In a certain time and in a certain lonely place, a traveler might have seen a golden braid of hair lying along the ground. If he followed the braid, he would arrive at a tower that had neither stair nor door, only a single, high window into which the braid disappeared. From the window floated the sound of plaintive singing.

A timid traveler would have passed this eerie prison by, but one young man did not. He was a prince, and the prisoner in the tower became his heart's delight.

The prisoner's name was Rapunzel, which in German means "rampion," or "bellflower," a plant with delicious, delicate leaves, and that plant sent Rapunzel to her tower.

Before Rapunzel's birth, her pregnant mother was filled with longing for the plant. As it happened, rampion was a rarity in the place where the mother lived: The only garden where it grew belonged to a witch, a jealous, powerful creature whom few saw – or wanted to see. Her rampion was imprisoned behind a high wall.

But the pregnant woman's craving for the rampion was so strong that her husband dared the witch's wrath. In the night, he scaled the wall and stole the plant for his wife. The taste only

made her pining stronger, so the husband went to the garden again and yet again. One night as he bent to cut the plant, his wrist was grasped by a bony, clawlike hand, and he heard the voice of the witch. She hissed that both the man and his wife would die for the theft unless they made reparation. In the end, the man promised the witch the couple's unborn child to save their lives. When the birth took place, the witch claimed her due. She took the infant girl away and named her for the plant that had been her price.

Rapunzel was a golden child, and the witch loved her in a grasping way. As years passed and Rapunzel blossomed, the witch shut Rapunzel in the tower to keep the girl for her own. Each day she bade Rapunzel let down her golden hair from the window, and each day she climbed this ladder to see her caged darling. Having no one else for company, Rapunzel had to be content. But she felt restless longings; and so, in her tower, she sang like a bird.

The plangent melody drew the prince. On the day that he found the tower, he heard the witch demand that Rapunzel's golden braid be lowered and saw the woman clamber up to the tower room. When the witch had left, the prince made the same demand. Rapunzel obediently let down her shining ladder for him. He came that day and the next and the next, and the girl grew to love him dearly.

The witch discovered the couple. Stricken, she cut Rapunzel's hair and banished her to a wilderness. Then she turned her sharp claws on the prince.

Alone in her wilderness, Rapunzel sang as before, mourning her lover. When a year had passed, he appeared before her, a wanderer in the dark, for the witch's claws had blinded him. Like a golden thread, Rapunzel's singing had drawn him to her. The tears she shed as she kissed his eyes cured the blindness. Together, then, they traveled to his father's kingdom, and there they lived for the rest of their lives, safe from the malice of the witch who knew no love but possession.

villages and hamlets among people who had known them all their lives, and unless caught in action, they might never betray their evil natures, although the superstitious thought there were signs.

Black witchcraft, for instance, was an expression of intrinsic malevolence, greed and destructiveness; therefore, it often was assumed that witches' bodies reflected their souls, that they resembled the bent-over, bad-tempered crones of whom every village had its share. Having animals other than the usual barnyard creatures inhabiting one's cottage could lead to suspicions of witchcraft, too: Witches habitually assumed the form of animals—hares, cats or ravens, for instance—in order to go about their business undetected. And those witches who derived their powers, like Doctor Faustus in Wittenberg, from pacts with Satan, were accompanied everywhere by familiars—demonic servants in the shapes of cats, toads, snakes, birds, even spiders or bees.

All told, it was risky to be an ill-formed, scolding, solitary old woman who kept a pet cat or toad (toads were not uncommon in dirt-floored village cottages) to ease the loneliness. Old women of that sort were likely to be shunned or even tormented by unkind or frightened neighbors; on the other hand, some of those old women were not above pretending to witchcraft to blackmail their neighbors with threats that produced gifts of food and money.

Meanwhile, real witches pursued their pastimes with impunity. Some, indeed, were old women, but others were simply healthy-looking housewives or even the housewives' rosy children.

Glimpses of such witch children could be charming, as in the tale of the Shetland housewife found standing at her door, brandishing the washing with which she was busy and loudly berating seven frantically mewing tabby kittens. They were her children, whom she had taught to shift shape; unfortunately, they could not recall the means of returning to human form. The woman turned them back into children and boxed their ears soundly for forgetting their lessons.

In truth, the discovery of witches—any witches—brought only grief to the innocent people who knew and perhaps loved them, and the case was especially hard when the witch was a child. The Irish tell a story of this sad kind, about a man who once lived happily with his wife and little daughter at Malin More, on the western coast of the island. One morning, this man went, as was his habit, to cut peat at a bog on the cliffs high above Donegal Bay. At noon, as she did every day, his wife sent their daughter to him with a wooden bowl of steaming broth to have for his lunch.

When the father saw the girl picking her way gingerly toward him and holding the bowl carefully in her small hands so that none of the hot broth would spill, he laid down his peat knife and went with a smile to meet her. Together they found a dry place where they could sit and look out to sea. A few minutes passed in companionable silence while the father ate his meal. Presently a ship appeared, making good speed on the green water of the bay.

"Oh, where is she going?" cried the girl.

The father squinted for a moment and replied, "To Killybegs, I'd say."

There was a pause and then the daughter, with a sly, sideways glance, said softly, "I can keep her from reaching there, just by wishing."

But the father only laughed indulgently and lighted his pipe.

While he smoked, the girl took his broth bowl and washed it in a little pool. When she had cleaned the bowl, she pushed it idly around in the water, dragging it slowly to the edge of the pool. At length she said to her father, "Now look at the ship, and see what I have done." The father looked up. The ship, instead of beating toward Drumanoo Head, which hid the mouth of the river that led to Killybegs, was heading swiftly toward the jagged cliffs below them.

"When the ship is only a little nearer the cliffs," said the girl, "I shall turn this bowl over and it will sink, and the very same thing will happen to that pretty ship at sea." She rocked the bowl with one hand. The ship heeled far over on its side, although it was running before the wind. Then the girl smiled at her father with a bright, secret smile.

He was a good man, and the first thing he said was, "Let her be, daughter."

The little girl shrugged, smiled her stranger's smile again and carefully plucked the bowl from the pool. She dried it on her apron. The white-sailed ship slowly changed course and headed up the coast toward Drumanoo Head.

"Where did you learn this thing?" said the father at last.

A silent spy

Spinner of webs, an archtrickster, and a silent and murderous trapper, the spider was tiny enough to hide in the hood of a witch's cloak as a familiar and whisper instruction in her ear.

Ordinary folk said that to dream of a spider meant betrayal. To see one in the morning brought bad luck, and to kill one summoned rain. The sight of spiders terrified wedding parties because the creatures were omens of unhappy marriage. And in Switzerland it was said that the plague, with its black sores, was spread by malevolent spiders traveling in secret from house to house.

"Oh, my mother is teaching me her craft," answered his daughter. "I learned it at my mother's knee." And taking the bowl, she walked demurely toward the cottage where they lived, with never a backward glance.

That is how a good man lost his happiness and his home. The wife he loved and trusted and the little daughter who was the apple of his eye both were in league with evil, and he was a helpless, hoodwinked bystander in his own home. A taciturn man, he said nothing more to either wife or daughter. That night, when he finished his work, he took his clothing and some food and left that place forever.

The Irish tale is striking because innocent people rarely saw black witches actually at work: Black witchcraft was a secret art. To be sure, there were plenty of whispered rumors, just as there were whispers about solitary old crones and their pets.

It was widely reported in the Hertfordshire village of Little Gaddesden, for instance, that people who peered through the cottage window of a woman named Rosina Massey — a dubious pastime in the first place — would see unnerving sights indeed. Dame Massey, it was said, entertained herself by standing before her hearth, conducting with great skill and vivacity while her crockery, from the teapot to the cups and saucers, danced to her commands. It was also said that her three-legged stool did her chores, including the washing of that very crockery.

And in another hamlet, whose name has been lost, children refused to walk past the house of a certain old woman. This was partly because she was abusive to children, and partly because of the collection of pottery animals displayed in her window. Each time a child in that village died or disappeared — not uncommon occurrences in those days — the collection of animals increased by one.

But gossips' whispers and children's night-fears were only hearsay, after all, and sensible people tended to treat them as such. Slightly more reliable evidence of witchcraft was to be found in cottage herb gardens. A woman who grew quantities of such plants as deadly nightshade, monkshood, thorn apple and henbane was likely to fall under suspicion: All of those plants were poisons, and black witches often indulged in poisoning. All the plants played a part, too, in the ointments some witches used to aid their night-flying.

It is only fair to point out, however, that gardens containing such herbs might possibly have belonged to white witches: The juice of deadly nightshade berries could be made into eyedrops for fashionable ladies, to enlarge their pupils and give them a soft, doe-eyed look; monkshood was also known as wolfsbane because it could be used to kill those predators of sheep; and thorn apple and henbane were common weeds. Still, the presence of all the plants together was ominous.

So was the presence in a house of the paraphernalia of image magic. This magic worked — as it had at least since the time of the Assyrians, thousands of years before — according to the doctrine of sympathy. An effigy of a person was made, and through enchantment, endowed with the essence of that person; after that, anything done to the image would affect the person. (By the same principle, the Irish child witch had endowed a simple wooden bowl with the essence of the ship at sea.)

The most common objects used for image magic, as is well known, were small figures made of wax, which could be melted in fire or dissolved in water to cause slow wasting, or could be stuck with nails or pins to produce illnesses in various parts of the victim's body. But the figures were also made of clay or carved of wood or plaited from straw. And the images could also be used for innocent purposes, such as attempting to draw a yearned-for person's love to the magicworker.

Again, it should be kept in mind that many people who were not witches practiced – or made efforts to practice – image magic. In the year 975, according to Anglo-Saxon records, a Northamptonshire woman forfeited her property – and her life by drowning under London Bridge – for murdering one "Ælsi, Wulfstan's father," by sticking nails in an image of him. Sometimes, indeed, image magic was used against witches themselves. The presence of images, in short, meant only that magic was being attempted, not that a witch was at work. The only true sign that a

witch was somewhere close lay in the effects of her craft. When fishermen's boats foundered in freak storms, when inexplicable accidents occurred, when strange illnesses decimated a village, when farmers' crops withered in the field, when cows went dry and cream refused to turn to butter, then people looked for malice nearby. Often enough, by one means or another, people in small villages could trace the malice to its source, if the witch was a neighbor; or they could find a way to defeat it, if the witch was one of those who lived alone in the remote countryside or forest.

Of the malevolent effects of the witch's work, few were so extensively documented as her theft of milk and her disruption of buttermaking, and that is understandable. A good milk cow was worth more than almost anything else a farmer owned, and the loss of its milk might mean the loss of his family's health. For the witch, the milk or butter she could charm to herself meant pleasure in malicious action success-

A raucous-voiced herald

Sooty-feathered and harsh of voice, the crow was a fit familiar to witches, prized for its ability to fly and spy. Villagers feared this carrion eater, for it was a messenger of mortality. A fluttering crow around the window or one that flew thrice over the roof, croaking each time, meant Death was on his way. Simply to see the bird flying alone could bring bad luck, and crows rising in a flock from a wood sometimes presaged famine.

Snaring an earthbound demon

An aphrodisiac, inspirer of visions and aid to flying, the mandrake was the most potent of the many plants that figured in witchcraft; its role was of such antiquity that it was sometimes called Circe's Plant, after that ancestress of witches. But in addition to its value as a drug, the mandrake had a characteristic that gave it astonishing power — and made its harvest a perilous task.

It was not completely vegetable, scholars said. The knobby, forked, manlike root harbored a tiny spirit or demon; thus the Romans called the mandrake half-man. Those who dared the capture of the demon could expect great reward.

What made the capture difficult was the pain it inflicted on the plant, for when its root was torn from the ground, the mandrake gave a shriek so terrible that any creature within earshot was struck dead. Accordingly, a variety of rituals grew up to protect those who desired the mandrake.

The plant had to be harvested at night, when the baleful glow of its leaves made it easy to find. The herb gatherer stuffed his ears with wax and dug around the plant until he had freed all but the last threads of root. Then he — or she — looped a line around the base of the root and tied that line to the collar of a dog. He placed a scrap of meat or bread just out of range of the tethered animal and ran for his life. The dog, in lunging for the food, would tear the mandrake from its bed of earth. The plant and the demon it sheltered now belonged to the gatherer; the dog, of course, would be killed by the demonic scream.

Once acquired, the mandrake root was treasured, for if it was bathed in wine and wrapped in silk, the demon within it would speak, offering counsel and prophecy.

fully performed, as well as profit in the marketplace with little effort on her part.

There were innumerable methods of acquiring the milk. Some witches traveled to neighboring pastures or dairies in the form of butterflies and nursed the cows in this almost unnoticeable shape. (The name of the insect, in fact, comes from the practice.) Some, like the witch described earlier, traveled as hares or as hedgehogs or as cats.

A forest-dwelling Scottish witch called Madam Widecomb traveled as an elder tree. One night, the tree was seen near a cow byre, reaching its long branches toward the animals; the farmer's mother in that case threw coals on the tree, burning it severely and stopping the theft. Even household objects were put to use. In Saxony, witches stuck an axhead into a post and pumped the handle, thereby drawing milk from their neighbors' cows. A witch in Yorkshire drew her supply, appropriately enough, from the legs of a milking stool.

And another English witch, whose village is not recorded, had a capacious leather bag and a wicked sense of humor. The witch had placed the bag under an enchantment so that, morning and night, at her bidding, it moved of its own power to her neighbors' pastures, drained the cows and brought their milk to her. Eventually she was caught in the act by the goodmen of her village. They bound her hands and took her and her bag to their priest.

That particular priest seems to have been something of a skeptic, for he refused to believe the claim of his irate villagers. He ordered that the witch be unbound and that she prove her powers.

"Well, I will, priest," said the witch coolly. She set her leather bag on the road before her, where it lay in a shapeless heap. The witch stood over the bag, fixed it with a steady eye and recited a spell, which has not been preserved.

Then she said, "Walk, Bag!" The bag shuddered and rose, and, in a clumsy but determined sort of way, it began to shuffle down the road.

After it had gone a hundred yards, the priest had seen enough. He signaled for the witch to halt the bag.

"Stop, Bag!" she said simply. The bag collapsed in the dust and lay still.

Moved by curiosity, the priest determined to try the spell himself. He stood over the bag, recited the witch's spell and, as she had done, ordered, "Walk, Bag!"

Nothing happened. The bag remained where it was, a lifeless mound of leather in the road. The priest turned to the witch, raising his brows.

"Well, priest," she said in response to his look, "it is my bag. I have faith in the words I speak and in the power behind them. If you had the proper faith, the bag would walk for you, too, and suck cows as well. You must have faith," she added primly, "to move unmoving things." But she did not specify what power it was that commanded her faith.

The priest rather lamely ordered the witch to stop believing, and also to stop stealing milk. The former was unlikely, but the latter may well have occurred. Pragmatic villagers did sometimes come to terms with known witches, agreeing to supply milk or cream or fruit regularly in exchange for immunity. No one cared to risk an angered witch's wrath. Besides the danger it embodied, the fact of witchcraft was terrifying in itself: Evil witches had the power to alter the order of nature. This they did not because of scholarly curiosity, in the manner of Bacon, but for reasons of greed or perhaps out of a motiveless malignancy.

The greed and malice, in fact, were the source of the power of the black witch's famed Evil Eye. Just by looking at an object—a newborn infant, for instance, a witch could harm or kill it, and the harm came from the strength of her ill will. If one looked into the eyes of an evil witch, it was said, one saw only flat blankness. No

The Witch's Garden

Choked with plants that the rest of human-kind shunned, pervaded by the narcotic per-fumes of poisonous blossoms, a witch's gar-den embodied a perverse understanding of nature. By the light of the moon, the witch harvested her crop; in secret she compounded it into mixtures that could hurt and kill.

Witches often were poisoners. The needles and red berries of yew, so baneful that the ground the tree shaded was cracked and sterile, brought swift agony, then death. So did monkshood, with its lovely purple sprays of cowl-shaped flowers. Tinctures that bred fearful visions could be made from a variety of

plants: deadly nightshade, with sweet blue-black berries as large as cherries; henbane, with corpse gray, purple-veined flowers; and thorn apple, with chalice-shaped flowers of ghostly white. From hemlock, wreathed in tiny white flowers, oozed a juice that could make a man impotent; from roses, a distillation to entrap a reluctant lover.

No natural thing is essentially evil, but evil ends make evil means. Even flowers as innocent as water lilies could serve the black witch, for they figured in the ointments used for flying. The industrious bees that haunted a witch's garden served her ends, too: They made the wax from which the magicworker fashioned images to practice her arts upon.

111

The secret of flight

Few witches ascribed their powers of flight merely to the brooms, distaffs or farm implements that served as their nighttime steeds. The magical energy that transported them came partly from an ointment, thickly smeared over their bodies, that incorporated the most potent herbs in witchcraft: monkshood, henbane, deadly nightshade, mandrake and hemlock. Blended with other extracts in a base of lard – or, it was whispered, the fat of unbaptized children – the ingredients combined in a magical synergy so powerful that witches, by their own accounts, were spirited across entire countries in the twinkling of an eye.

welcoming reflection of the observer appeared in a witch's pupil.

Considering both the evil intent and the power to act on that intent, it is not surprising that witches attracted the attention of Satan, the Great Adversary. They were the perfect grist for his mill.

The two – prospective witch and Satanic master – struck their bargain in various ways, but the pact always was associated with borderlines, for the old power of in-between places or times had not been forgotten. In Scotland, for instance, a would-be witch had only to go on a night of the full moon to a lonely beach and place herself between the marks of the high and low tides. At midnight – the interstice between one day and the next, called the witching hour – she made three turns in the direction opposite that of the sun's path. It was a deliberate gesture inviting disorder.

Then she sat down, placed one hand on the crown of her head and one beneath the soles of her feet and intoned nine times the charm, "Take all that is between my two hands." From that time on, she was Satan's creature.

But most witches made their pacts at the festivals of the devil known as sabbats. (The name may have arisen either as a blasphemous mockery of the Christian Sabbath or from the Old French verb s'esbattre, meaning "to frolic.") Sabbats, it was said, took place in wild and lonely settings far from the curious and condemning eyes of civilization: Peaks such as the Brocken in Germany's Harz Mountains, the Bald Mountain near Kiev or the Puy-de-Dôme in the Auvergne, in France, all were famous sabbat sites. Sabbats occurred on the ancient borderline nights – the eves of May Day and Allhallows, as well as those of the equinoxes and solstices.

On those nights, good folk huddling safe in their houses heard the rush of the night wind outside or saw black shadows racing across the moon's silver face and knew that the witches were in flight. Flying was invariably the way witches and prospective witches traveled to their great gatherings. They coated their bodies with powerful ointments, mounted their steeds and raced along the narrow village lanes, breaking free to soar above the rooftops, past the steeples of the churches and high above the branches of the trees.

Broomsticks were not necessarily their vehicle of choice. Some witches, in fact, left their broomsticks – transformed to look like themselves – in their beds to fool their innocent husbands. Then they flew on hurdles—rectangular frames made of branches and used as temporary fencing for farm animals. Or they flew on rakes or forks or shovels.

Some witches had magic bridles; in Scandinavia, these were fashioned from the bones and flayed skin of fresh corpses and called *gand-reid* bridles, meaning the bridles of supernatural beings. Flung over the head of an unsuspecting person or animal, the bridles made that human or beast fly as long and as far as the witch commanded. The expression "hag-ridden," applied to people or beasts who appeared to be exhausted when morning came, derived from that practice.

When the various witches and witches-to-be converged on their destination, they joined a frenzied orgy of chanting and dancing and drinking presided over by the Great Adversary himself. The central act for each witch or aspiring witch was obeisance to evil. Each person vowed her soul to Satan, and to seal the bargain she gave her body to him, to use however he pleased before the eyes of all her fellows.

Or so it was whispered. No innocent person ever saw a sabbat, although those who ventured out on Midsummer Eve sometimes heard the high fluting of music pipes and the demanding stutter of beating drums. When morning came and the world began to stir, however, the celebrants of the sabbat were in their normal guises again, back among ordinary people, going with apparent innocence about their ordinary tasks.

But they were not innocent at all. They were part of a secret sisterhood now. "Witches always know one another," went a saying on the Isle of Wight. "They pass on the lane without a glance or a word or a nod, but as they pass, each gives a soft little laugh." And they were in the position to get whatever they wanted and avenge any suspected slight, no matter how small, with little risk of blame.

Servants of Satan, the witches had servants themselves. These were their familiars, the demonic agents given by the devil. The pet cat purring before a fire, the crow perched in the sun on a windowsill, the toad or snake on the cool cottage floor, the hare in the garden, even the spider, spinning its lacy web, could listen and talk and do the witch's bidding. The familiars could spy on the activities of the neighbors, bringing back useful gossip to while away an evening; they could rob the orchard and the dairy and the brewing crock. They could even maim or kill.

Their mistresses pampered these clever pets, feeding them on the very best table scraps and even, it is said, dressing them in velvet garments when the weather was cold. They also protected them, and for that reason, it was dangerous to harm an animal, as country people knew. Sometimes the response to such an act was little more than a warning.

In Somerset once, for instance, there lived an old woman who kept three pet toads with the engaging names of Duke, Dick and Merryboy. One autumn afternoon, carrying her toads in a basket to keep her company, she watched three young farmers reap a field, singing to the rhythm of their flashing scythes. One of

the toads hopped from the basket directly into the path of the reapers. The young men sniggered and, before the woman's horrified eyes, slashed the beast to pieces.

"I'll set hell on you," cried the woman. "None of you will finish this day's work." And, having said that curse, she trudged off across the field, carrying the remaining toads carefully away.

The young men only laughed, but within moments one of them had cut his hand with his scythe badly enough to stop his working. The next sliced across the toe of his boot on a downswing, and the last cut his boot open from one side to the other. Unnerved, they left the field. As their neighbor had said, none of them finished work that day.

It was a useful lesson for the farmers, and one that could have been much harsher. In the Lake District, for example, there lived a witch whose cat was killed by the innkeeper's dog. The old woman stood by, sad but dry-eyed (witches could not weep) while the innkeeper's servant dug a grave for the animal. The old woman asked the servant, whose name was Willan, to read some verses over the cat from a book she had, a request that sent the man into howls of laughter. He threw the small, furry body into the hole he had dug, reciting in a loud voice a silly, mocking rhyme: "Ashes to ashes and dust to dust. Here's a hole and go thou must."

"Very well," said the old woman bitterly. "You will be punished, as you will see."

And Willan was indeed punished. A day later, as he was plowing the innkeeper's field, the plowshare caught in a rock on the ground; the handles flew up into the air and pierced the young man's eyes. He was blinded for life.

Incidents of this kind were repeated endlessly, and all tell the same tale – of rural greed and petty malice, of aimless evildoing and fierce revenge. Set apart by her enmity for her fellows, the witch led a mean and violent life and, as often as not, met a mean and violent end. For instance, traveling in animal form was a convenience, but it entailed risk – animals were vulnerable to the weapons of hunters and to the teeth and claws of stronger beasts.

The cruelty of the witches' lives and deaths was nowhere seen so clearly as in the rugged islands off the Scottish coast and in the Highlands, where the mountain winds moaned and wuthered all year long. In this bleak land, the cries of wheeling curlews carried far, and the belling of stags in autumn echoed loudly across the slopes. The summers were short and unpredictable, the winters long and dark.

The region produced a race of men who were hardy and dour. Their hatred and fear of their witches was remarkable, even for that time, and the witches returned the enmity in full measure.

A tale of that era relates how the Highland witches sought revenge against two men renowned for their detestation and pursuit of the sisterhood. The first man was John Macgillichallum – called in Gaelic *Iain Garbh*, or "Rugged John," for his bravery. He lived on Raasay, an island sheltered between the Isle of Skye and the mainland. One autumn day, Macgillichallum and his men set sail for the island of Lewes, fifty miles to the northwest, to hunt deer. The morning was cold and bright and clear, the sky as blue as gentian and the high-piled clouds as white as cream. Waves sparkled around his boat as Rugged John sailed away.

He was never seen alive again. Conflicting tales about his death arose later, but little was really known. The shining day led to a night of squalls and screaming winds and another day as bad. On that second day, seamen at the Point of Aird on Skye saw the little boat beating toward them through the storm. They saw its drunken lurching in the waves and heard across the water the shouts of the men on board. And they said – the few who would talk about the incident later – that through the winds' wail and the sheets of rain and boiling sea mist they heard another sound and saw another sight in the moments before the boat capsized and sank. The sound they heard was the angry howling of dozens of cats, and the sight they saw was the lean and shadowy shapes of the cats themselves, crawling along the gunwales, clawing up the mast and swarming through the cockpit around Macgillichallum and his men.

The night of that day found the second man the witches hated secluded in a hunting hut in the desolate forest of Gaich, in the Inverness district called Badenoch. This man was called the Hunter of the Hills, perhaps for his prowess in the forest, and perhaps for his pursuit of the mountain witches. He sat with his deerhounds before a crackling fire, while the icy rain beat against the window and the wind screamed outside.

A pair of sinuous helpers

Anciently inimical to each other, the serpent and the cat were favorites of witches. The serpent seems to have played the smaller role: While it could serve as a familiar, it was chiefly valued for its fearful aspect and its link to Satan – useful in repelling the curious, who might interfere with a witch's business. To dream of a serpent signified that someone had a grudge against the dreamer.

The cat, on the other hand, was surrounded by speculation. Its pupils – narrow slits in the daytime and luminous black globes at night – linked it to the moon and emphasized its power to see into the future. Cats were said to suck the breath from infants at night. And cats forecast the weather: When they scampered and cavorted, wind was on its way; when they washed their ears, rain was coming; when they sat with their backs to the fire, they awaited frost and storms.

Except in northern England, where it was thought lucky to own a black cat (but unlucky to meet a strange one), black cats were the most common embodiments of Satan. As for cats that served as familiars – rather than as transformations of the witches themselves – they were usually brindled.

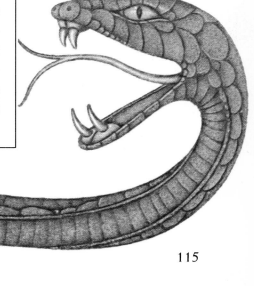

B. Berg

Michael Herr fuuent.

Each eve before the seasons changed, prudent folk stayed close to home, and in the watches of the night they spoke of flocks of witches, gone to dance in raging revelries and please themselves with frightful rites.

The door blew open. The hunter saw a cat huddled on the step, its fur soaked and matted, its meager little body trembling. The dogs sprang snarling to their feet. They would have killed it, but the hunter called them off.

He did so, he later said, because the cat had spoken, asking for a mercy he could not deny. It said that it was a witch who had renounced the craft and fled to him for safety from the vengeful hunting of its sister witches.

He brought the cat in and set it before the fire to warm while he thought what to do. But it behaved as innocently as a real cat might. It washed its coat industriously as it dried and its fur fluffed, and said nothing for half an hour or more. Then it settled down before the flames, tucking its paws in for warmth and wrapping its tail neatly around its body. It began to purr. The dogs twitched nervously, but they let the little animal be.

Soothed by the heat of the fire and the rhythmic rumbling of the cat, the hunter began to drowse. The rain still beat outside, but all was quiet within. Suddenly, however, the hunter's eyes snapped open. His dogs were on their feet, bristling and growling.

The cat was gone. In its place on the hearth, placidly smiling, stood a much-loved woman of his own village, who was called the Goodwife of Laggan.

"You are a gullible man, Hunter," she said. "John Macgillichallum the witch hater is dead this day. Macgillichallum lies five fathoms down, my sisters say, and the fish are nibbling at his eyes. And your time has come, too."

She sprang for his throat, her long fingernails curled and the breath hissing through her shining teeth. But the dogs were quicker. They knocked the woman to the ground. The minutes that followed were a welter of smoking blood and screaming animals. The dogs tore off the woman's breast; she laid their bellies open with her nails. Then there was silence, save for the whimpering of the injured dogs and the flapping of a crow's wings outside the hut. The woman had vanished and the dogs were dying.

All this the hunter told his wife the following day, when he reappeared in his village, grim-faced and bearing the bodies of his hounds. He heard from his wife what he expected to hear: The Goodwife of Lag-

gan lay in her bed; she had been taken desperately ill the night before, and the villagers despaired of her life.

Without saying a word, the hunter left his wife and strode swiftly through the village lanes to the cottage where the woman lived, for there was still one more thing he had to do.

He reached the place in short order. The door stood open to reveal the firelit chamber and the quiet, plaid-shawled figures of the women of the village. They were busy about the hearth, warming blankets and brewing tea from sweet-smelling herbs that might save their neighbor's life.

The good women clustered around him when he entered, hushing the male intruder in the sick woman's chamber.

"It is a chill she caught, and she is old and frail," said one of them, and would have turned him out. He shouldered her aside and pushed to the bed where the small figure lay, making hardly a ripple in the thick mound of bedclothes. Her face was as white as the white braids that framed it, and her eyes were closed.

"How is it with you, Servant of Satan?" said the Hunter of the Hills to the Goodwife of Laggan.

She made no reply, and his neighbors fluttered angrily around him, so many protective hens with one fragile chick. But the hunter tore the bedclothes and the concealing gown away, and showed the bloody marks of his hounds' teeth and told his story.

When the hunter was done, the goodwife spoke. In a failing voice, she told the

Belled and beribboned dancers

Ugly and venomous though it was, the toad seems to have been among the most cherished of witch familiars: The creatures were dressed in velvet by their mistresses, ornamented with bells and encouraged to dance.

Common folk both feared and valued them. Toads were burned because the horns on their foreheads marked them as agents of Satan and because witches used toad spittle to concoct ointments that conferred invisibility. On the other hand, toads were admired for their ability to hear distant thunder long before the human ear could catch it; the sight of the little creatures making their way to safe water provided a reliable indicator of approaching storms. And very elderly toads — rarely glimpsed — carried precious jewels in their heads, effective antidotes to poison.

A cache of charms

With knots, images and charms, witches focused and heightened their powers. As a witch murmured her incantations, she could strengthen a spell by fashioning a witch's ladder – nine feathers knotted into a multicolored cord to form a kind of perverted rosary. A peacock feather, with its ocular ornament, cast the curse of the evil eye on anyone to whom it was given, dooming the recipient to a slow, wasting death. And a wax or clay image of an enemy, mutilated or burned, or a charm bag containing coffin nails and, often, hair or nail parings from the intended victim, also could transmit a deadly spell.

But other charms – often from the store of a white witch – averted evil. For protection against malevolence, people carried a medallion bearing the mystic slogan abracadabra, or a magical stone such as amber, bloodstone or lodestone, or a bracelet of naturally pierced pebbles culled from a streambed. These small objects had healing powers, it was thought. Amber shrank goiters; bloodstone could stanch either internal or external bleeding; and magnetic lodestone banished dull melancholy. And just as the magical word on the abracadabra charm dwindled to a single letter at each apex of the design, so the charm itself could cause a fever to abate.

Some talismans could do more than just fend off evil. A young man intent on worldly success might pin a parchment image signifying fortune to his cap, while a spurned lover might melt a wax heart in hopes of softening the unyielding heart of his beloved.

truth about the bargain she had made and the damage she had done. She felt death coming, she said, and in her head she heard the distant hoofbeats of the master who would claim her.

"There is a way you may be saved," the hunter said. He told her what it was and, having done his duty, departed. The village wives trailed silently after him, leaving the Witch of Laggan alone to die.

The rest of the tale was told by two travelers who that night were heading for the Badenoch lands through the forests of the Monadhliath Mountains, a few miles to the north. The way was hard, the night dark and rainy, and the two men walked with swift strides, keeping to the middle of the track.

"Stop a moment," one said suddenly. They stopped, and both heard ahead of them, through the whisper of the rain and the rustle of the branches, a high, breathless moaning. Then from the shadows on the track ahead emerged a figure of a woman dressed in black, the bosom of her gown soaking, and her white braids flecked with blood. She hesitated for a moment when she reached them, peering up into their faces, panting and chattering with fear.

"Is this the track that leads to Dalarossie Churchyard?" she said.

"It is," answered one man, and both men turned to watch the woman as, without another word, she set off down the road, running with a shambling gait and turning again to peer back over her shoulder. She reached the place where the road crested over a hill and vanished from view, and all the men heard then was the whisper

of the rain again. Unnerved, the travelers glanced at each other and began to walk, more briskly than before. But after a few moments they paused once more and drew to the side of the track.

Loping toward them at an easy pace were two long-legged black hounds. Their heads swung from side to side as they snuffled the ground, following a scent with apparent ease. They passed the travelers with no more than a glance and vanished behind them, where the road crested over the hill.

Before the men could move, a hooded rider on a black horse came into view, following the hounds. He drew rein beside the men. Two eyes glittered from the depths of the hood; a burning stench hovered in the air.

"Is this the road to Dalarossie Churchyard?" a soft voice asked.

"It is."

"And did a woman pass by you not long ago?"

"She did."

The rider turned away from the travelers, touched the horse's flank with one spurred heel and passed swiftly on. At the road's crest, he, too, disappeared.

Now the travelers put their backs into it and trudged along the track with as much speed as they could muster. They spoke not at all, for they were very frightened indeed, and they did not care for the company on that road.

Dalarossie Churchyard, at Strathdearn, where the travelers had come from, was famous in those parts. It was a sanctuary for the living, as all churchground was. But that ground had possessed singular

power for centuries: It was a sanctuary for the newly dead, too. Any just-released soul, no matter how smirched, was safe from Satan's grasp at Dalarossie. For that reason, men or women who were dying sometimes had their pallets carried there when the end neared.

An hour passed and then another, and the travelers walked steadily on. At last behind them they heard the hoofs of the rider, but they did not look around.

He drew rein beside them, however, and the soft voice said with satisfaction, "She was just at the gate. It was easy for the dogs."

Slung like a limp doll across his saddle, white braids trailing in the mud, was the black-gowned figure of the Witch of Laggan, her back broken, her body bloodied and bitten beyond recognition. The travelers told their tale in Badenoch, and the listeners heard them with relief. If they had had the body, they would have buried it deep, face downward so that when the witch's corpse began to dig its way out, as sometimes happened, it would dig into the earth and not into the fresh air above. The Hunter of the Hills said nothing. But that night and every other of his life, he listened to the wind and kept an eye out for black shadows streaking across the moon, mindful of the hatred that the Witch of Laggan's sisters bore him. All of this was long ago.

As the centuries rolled by and cities grew where villages had stood, the witches retreated from humankind. They lived on for a while in deep forests and other unvisited places, practicing their sorceries in solitude. Memories of them continued to stir the fears of people for a while, but at last even the memories became no more than bedtime tales to frighten children.

But some people with a taste for enchantment remembered always the witches' great forebears. Hidden from men's sight but not forgotten, Vainamöinen and Manannan and Merlin—and Gwydion, perhaps, and also Math the Ancient—all waited, patient spirits whose day to act would certainly come again. 🐍

Baba Yaga traveled in a mortar, rowing the air with a pestle and sweeping her tracks away with a broom.

haunter of the Birch Forest

Deep in a birch forest in the heart of Russia was a small clearing, and in that clearing lived the witch Baba Yaga, meager as a skeleton and always hungry. Everything around her had to do with food. Her crooked little hut perched high on a giant chicken leg, and the fence around the hut was built from human bones, left over from her messy meals. When Baba Yaga went hunting, she traveled in a mortar, rowing the air with a pestle and sweeping her tracks away with a broom. She lived a solitary life, as might be expected, for few cared to risk her eager grasp and ever-blazing oven. Still, even Baba Yaga had occasional visitors, mostly straying travelers, and some of her visitors lived to tell the tale. One of these was no more than a timid girl.

This is how the adventure came about. At the edge of Baba Yaga's forest lived an ugly, evil-tempered woman with her two equally ugly, evil-tempered daughters and, to the woman's chagrin, her one lovely stepdaughter, Vasilisa. Vasilisa's father was a merchant who had married the woman after his first wife's death and then—driven no doubt by the tenor of his new spouse's conversation—traveled far away on business, leaving his sweet-natured daughter in her care.

The girl's lot was a hard one. Her stepmother banished her to a cold and lonely attic room. Her jealous stepsisters made no se-

cret of their dislike, and what is worse, they used her as a servant. Vasilisa was required to tend the pigs and weed the garden, clean the house and cook the meals, and from these meals she was given only the meanest scraps. Curiously enough, however, she flourished and bloomed, pretty as a rose among the thorns.

Vasilisa thrived because her own mother, on her deathbed, had given her a magical doll. It was a tiny creature with glowing eyes, and it was alive. Vasilisa kept it near her always, as her mother had said to do, and she told no one of its existence. The doll did the sweeping and polishing, the cooking and gardening, so the growing girl could rest. In return, Vasilisa petted and fed it. At night, when the girl was locked in her room, the doll kept her company.

As the years passed and the maidens in the household approached marriageable age, the stepmother found herself rankled by the very sight of Vasilisa, whose charming face presented an unwelcome contrast to the appearance of her own dull daughters. Eventually, the stepmother decided to rid herself of the girl.

Accordingly, one autumn evening she set tasks for all three maidens: Her own daughters were to knit and make lace, Vasilisa to spin, and all this fine work was to be done by the light of one candle. Obediently, the maidens bent over their work.

Daylight departs early in the Russian autumn, and soon the candle made only a tiny pool of light in the shadowy room where the three girls worked. After a while, the elder stepsister—pretending to trim the candle wick—snuffed out even that feeble light, just as she had been instructed by her mother.

At once, there occurred an event so strange that it has not been explained from that day to this, although it appears to have been

the work of Vasilisa's stepmother, and she must have had magical aid
to do it. It was as if a spell had been cast upon the house. Every candle
guttered and died. Every room was dark and so silent that the maidens clearly heard the rustlings of a mouse, busy at work behind the
walls. The elder stepsister—as her mother had told her to do—turned
spitefully on Vasilisa, just as if the pretty girl had caused this calamity.

"Now," she said, "this house will be without a light unless we get
it from Baba Yaga in the forest, and how will you finish the task our
mother set for you? I need not go: I can see to work by the moonlight on my lacemaking pins. My sister need not go: She can work by
the moonlight on her knitting needles. But no light reflects from
your spindle. Since you cannot see to work, you can make yourself
useful by going to Baba Yaga and bringing back a light for us." And
she leaped up and thrust Vasilisa from the room.

Vasilisa slowly climbed the stairs to her attic, where the magic
doll quietly waited. She fed the doll the scraps she had saved for it and
cried, "Help me, dolly. My father is not here to save me and my
stepsisters are sending me to Baba Yaga. She is death itself."

The doll's eyes shone like two candles. It appeared to consider
the dilemma for a moment. Then it said calmly in its tiny voice, "Do as
you are told, Vasilisa, but take me in your pocket. No harm will be-
fall you while I am with you."

So Vasilisa took the doll, put it in the pocket of her apron and
slipped from the house into the forest, picking her way as quickly as
she could among the gleaming white trunks of the birch trees. The
moon sailed overhead, its light casting curious shapes in Vasilisa's
path. As she walked, she saw the eyes of forest creatures glittering in
the shadows, and she heard strange rustlings and murmurings.

Suddenly a pale horseman galloped across her path, white-faced, wearing white and riding a white horse.

Once she heard a deep, low growl. No harm came to her, however.

The night wore on and the moon set. Vasilisa shivered with the cold, but still she walked. Suddenly a pale horseman galloped across her path, white-faced, wearing white and riding a white horse. He disappeared into the forest. A silvery light crept through the trees behind him, and at that moment, the first bird sang.

Now Vasilisa walked through a waking forest. After an hour another rider flew by. This one was a red-faced man, clothed in blazing scarlet and mounted upon a roan. Behind him a shaft of rosy sunlight shone through the leaves. The air began to warm.

Still Vasilisa walked alone, save for the doll in her pocket. She walked the whole day, and as the light began to slant through the trees and the shadows to lengthen, she came upon a clearing. She halted at once in the shelter of the birches, for what she saw was fearful indeed. In the clearing stood a high fence made of silvery bones, and on each fence post grinned an empty-eyed skull. The gate was made of bones, too, but the lock was a sharp-toothed mouth and the bolt a skeletal hand. Within the fence was the witch's house, rocking gently on its chicken leg. No one was there.

As Vasilisa stared, a black-cloaked rider on a sable horse swept across the clearing and vanished into the trees. Behind him streamed smoky fingers of darkness that curled around the bone fence and shadowed the house. As night fell, the eyes of the fence-post skulls began to glow like torches, casting double beams of firelight on the ground around the fence.

The clearing was very still after the horseman passed by, but as Vasilisa waited among the trees she began to hear faraway the faint sounds of branches crackling and leaves rustling. The noises

After an hour, another rider flew by, clothed in blazing scarlet and mounted upon a roan.

sounded nearer and nearer, and then out of the wood swept Baba Yaga, riding in her mortar, with her pestle in one hand and her broom in the other. She alighted before the gate, her long nose quivering in the cool evening air. "I smell Russian blood," she said in a thin, reedy voice. "Come out, whoever hides here." Vasilisa felt in her pocket to make sure the doll was with her, then stepped from the sheltering branches and bowed before the witch.

"It is I, Vasilisa." The girl spoke shyly and kept her eyes politely lowered. "My stepsisters have sent me for light."

"Indeed. I know of your stepsisters," said Baba Yaga with an unpleasant smile. "You shall have light, and you might even live to take it home. But first you must live here and work for me. Unlock. Open up," she added to the gate, which did so at once.

Vasilisa followed the witch through the gate, which shut behind her with a rattle of bones and a click of the lock. The mortar, pestle and broom that the witch had used whisked themselves out of sight, and Vasilisa followed Baba Yaga up a ladder into the hut. Then Baba Yaga threw herself into a chair. Her eyes glittered. "I'm hungry," she said. "Serve me everything you find in the oven."

In the oven Vasilisa found a roast suckling pig and in the pantry pickled mushrooms and *kasha*, salt herring, *bliny* with butter, *borscht* and the little pastries called *pirozhki* as well as wine—enough food for at least ten people. All of it she served the witch, who ate with gusto and at length. Finally she wiped her mouth and announced: "Tomorrow I am going out. In the wooden bin in the yard is a bushel of wheat; sort it from the chaff. Sweep the yard. Clean the hut until not a speck of dirt remains. Wash all the linen, and make sure that it is as white as new-fallen snow. Then cook me a fine big dinner. If all

As Vasilisa stared, a black-cloaked rider on a sable horse swept across the clearing and vanished into the trees.

this isn't done, and done well, I'll grind your bones." And she closed her eyes and began to snore.

Vasilisa crept into a corner with the scraps of food the witch had left, and fed them carefully to the doll. She wept at the impossible task the witch had set for her and at the prospect of becoming the witch's dinner, but the doll was not at all perturbed. Its eyes shone comfortingly, and it said in its little voice, "The morning is wiser than the evening. Go to sleep, Vasilisa the Beautiful, and fear not."

When Vasilisa awoke early the next morning, the glowing eyes of the skulls were fading to blankness. The white horseman and then the red galloped through the clearing, light streaming behind them, and the day broke. Baba Yaga awoke and whistled for her mortar and pestle, which appeared, along with the broom. The witch hopped into the mortar, favored Vasilisa with an ominous and long-toothed grin, and swept away, leaving the girl to her tasks.

But the doll was ready. It leaped from Vasilisa's pocket and washed the clothing, hanging it neatly up to dry and whiten in the sunshine. It cleaned the hut, swept the yard and raked the dirt into neat patterns. Vasilisa had nothing to do but cook the dinner and examine the witch's hut, which she did with curiosity, admiring the embroideries and chests full of silver, and avoiding mysterious jars and bottles and jugs of strange liquids. As the day drew to a close, the doll settled down to the wheat bin and with its nimble little fingers winnowed the grain from the chaff.

Eventually the black horseman swept by, the skulls' eyes began to gleam, and Vasilisa heard the far-off rustlings that heralded the witch's arrival. Then in came Baba Yaga, looking ravenous.

"Everything done?" said the witch.

"Yes, indeed," said Vasilisa. "Please see for yourself." Baba Yaga marched through the hut to inspect it, growing more morose with each piece of tidily folded snowy linen and each neatly scrubbed pot. She clearly was disappointed, but all she said was, "Faithful servants, grind my wheat." At once, three pairs of hands appeared, gathered up the wheat and disappeared again.

The evening passed much as had the one before: The witch ate a gargantuan meal and set the girl another round of tasks for the following day, the worst of which was to separate all the dust particles from a barrelful of poppy seeds. Then, after reminding Vasilisa that failing at any of the tasks would mean death, she arranged herself for sleep and soon was snoring peacefully away.

Trapped in the dreadful hut within the bony fence, Vasilisa spent a second anxious night, listening to the rumblings of the sleeping Baba Yaga and fearing both the darkness and the coming dawn. In the morning, however, Baba Yaga simply disappeared with her mortar and pestle into the forest as before.

The doll set to work to fulfill all the tasks and separate the dust from the poppy seeds. By nightfall, when the black horseman rode by again, the skulls' eyes gleamed again and the witch returned, the seeds were clean. Baba Yaga made no comment to the girl. She only cried, "Faithful servants, grind these seeds to get their oil." And the three pairs of hands materialized out of the air as before and disappeared with the pile of poppy seeds.

Still, Baba Yaga seemed in a benevolent frame of mind, for her. After her huge dinner she seemed in need of entertainment. She glanced at Vasilisa and said, "You've certainly been dull and quiet up until now. You may ask a question, if you are curious enough and brave enough. I will warn you in fairness, however, that not every question has the answer you might wish for."

Vasilisa gathered her courage and said, "Baba Yaga, I want to ask about the three riders I saw on my journey."

"It's as well for you that you thought to ask only about things outside this hut," the witch replied with her nasty grin. "I don't like young maidens who pry into my private affairs. Very well, here is an answer for you. Those riders are my faithful servants all. The pale man on the pale horse is my daybreak, the red man on the roan is my sun, and the black rider my night.

"And now it's my turn," she continued. "How did you manage to do the tasks I set for you?"

"By my mother's blessing," replied the girl timidly. But she need not have been frightened: Baba Yaga had a profound dislike of any blessing. With a snarl she jumped from her chair and pushed Vasilisa out of the house and through the gate. She snatched a skull from the fence, stuck it on a pole and thrust it into Vasilisa's hand. "A little light for your sisters," she explained. "Now go away."

The journey home was dreadful. Trees clustered in her path and—as before—she saw glimmerings in the underbrush and heard strange noises. She kept a firm grasp on the pole that bore the skull, however, and its eyes gleamed steadily, lighting Vasilisa's way for her. The skull itself made not a sound.

When day broke, the eyes faded to emptiness. Vasilisa walked on through the forest until dusk, when at last she found herself at her stepmother's house again. The house was dark; not a light shone from any of the windows. Still, it was just twilight and not quite time to light the candles. Thinking that her stepmother and sisters

The eyes of the skull gleamed steadily, lighting the way for her, but the skull itself made not a sound.

would have no use for it, Vasilisa made to throw the skull away. A deep voice from within it stopped her.

"Do not cast me away," said the skull. "I am meant for your step-mother and sisters, and you must take me to them."

So Vasilisa pushed open the door of the house and went inside, bearing the skull. To her surprise, the three women within greeted her with pleasure, the first welcome she ever had had in that house. The reason for their unusual courtesy, it turned out, was the thing that had happened in Vasilisa's absence. If the stepmother had indeed used magic to douse her household's light, she had gotten more than she bargained for: No light at all could be made in the house. Even torches borrowed from neighbors guttered and died as soon as they were carried across the threshold. The women turned eagerly to the skull, whose eyes had begun to glow.

The gaze of those eyes—for gaze it now seemed—fell on the step-mother, who gave a cry and jumped aside. At once the light in the skull's eyes flared greedily. Of its own accord, the creature's head turned so that it again looked on the stepmother. In a moment she was enveloped in flame, and in another, entirely consumed. The eyes sought each of the stepsisters in turn and burned them to ashes. Then the light within the skull faded, and the room was quiet.

Left alone with the magical doll and the skull, Vasilisa waited out the night, pondering what to do next. She could not stay on alone in that unhappy house on the edge of Baba Yaga's forest. She decided to seek protection until her father should return from his travels and claim her for his own once more.

In the morning, therefore, she carefully buried the skull in the earth, gathered her clothing into a bundle and locked up the house. Then Vasilisa tucked her faithful doll into the pocket of her apron and walked to the nearest village. There she met an old woman so gentle and kindly looking that Vasilisa found the courage to tell her tale. This woman, being childless and, moreover, charmed by the girl's beauty and sad story, took Vasilisa in to live at her little cottage.

The old woman treated Vasilisa kindly—so kindly, in fact, that the girl found time hanging heavy on her hands. She asked the woman for flax to spin, and when she had it, set to work. Vasilisa's spinning was faster than lightning, and the thread she spun was as silky as her own hair. It was so very fine that no loom delicate enough for weaving it could be found, and no one in the village was skilled enough to make one. No one, that is, except the doll, who, one night while Vasilisa slept, made a loom from an old comb, a shuttle and the hairs from a horse's mane.

Vasilisa was delighted, and by the end of the winter had finished weaving her linen. It was so fine a fabric that it could be passed through the eye of a needle, and with the old woman's help, Vasilisa bleached it to perfect whiteness.

"Sell this linen," said Vasilisa to her protectress, "and keep the money for yourself. It seems only a fair payment for your kindness to me." But that good soul had better ideas. The linen, she thought, was too fine for anyone but the Tsar, and she set out for his palace, bearing the treasure.

She arrived in short order, and found the palace courtyard crowded with courtiers. They paid her no attention, being busy with affairs more important than whatever a poor old woman might want. Taking advantage of this, she unwrapped her beautiful linen and walked up and down the courtyard. The Tsar happened to glimpse her from a window. His curiosity aroused, he ordered her brought to him and so saw the enchanting fabric.

"How much do you want for this, grandmother?" he asked her with great kindness.

But the woman replied that she could not sell it, for it was too fine to be anything but a gift. So the Tsar took it. No one in the palace, however, dared hurt the gossamer stuff by sewing it into shirts, and in the end, he summoned the old woman again.

"If you can spin and weave such stuff," he said, "surely you can sew it into shirts for me."

"It was not I who spun and wove, but a girl I sheltered," said the woman, for she was honest as well as kind.

"Then let her sew the shirts."

And that is what happened. The old woman took the linen home to her village and told Vasilisa of the Tsar's command. With a smile Vasilisa obeyed: She locked herself in a room and cut her linen to make twelve fine shirts, which she sewed with stitches so small that they were invisible. The shirts were given to the Tsar, who found them so beautiful that he straightaway sent for the seamstress.

Vasilisa was brought to the court and to the Tsar. He was captivated at once by her beauty, then charmed by her goodness; in short, the Tsar fell in love with Vasilisa the Beautiful, and nothing would do but that she marry him. She did that very happily, of course, and all her trials were over for good: She had an imperial palace to live in, a hundred servants to do her bidding and the Tsar of All the Russias to love her.

But Vasilisa the Beautiful kept the magical doll safe in her pocket for the rest of her life.

Vasilisa was brought to the court and to the Tsar. He was captivated at once by her beauty, then charmed by

...oodness; in short, the Tsar fell in love with Vasilisa the Beautiful, and nothing would do but that she marry him.

Bibliography

Afanasév, Aleksandr Nikolaevich, *Russian Folk Tales*. Transl. by Robert Chandler. Shambhala/Random House, 1980.*

Arnason, Jón, *Icelandic Legends*. Transl. by George E. J. Powell and Eiríkur Magnússon. Richard Bentley, 1864.

Bates, Paul A., *Faust: Sources, Works, Criticism*. Harcourt, Brace & World, 1969.

Benét, William Rose, *The Reader's Encyclopedia*. 2nd ed. Harper & Row, 1965.

Bergen, Fanny D., ed., *Animal and Plant Lore*. Reprint. Kraus Reprint Co., 1969.

Bianchini, Francesco, and Francesco Corbetta, *Health Plants of the World: Atlas of Medicinal Plants*. Newsweek Books, 1977.

Blakeley, John D., *The Mystical Tower of the Tarot*. Robinson & Watkins Books, 1974.

Boase, Wendy, *The Folklore of Hampshire and the Isle of Wight*. Rowman and Littlefield, 1976.

Branston, Brian, *Gods of the North*. The Vanguard Press, no date.

Briggs, Katharine:
British Folktales. Pantheon Books, 1977.
A Dictionary of British Folk-Tales in the English Language, Vol. 2, Pt. A. Routledge & Kegan Paul, 1970.
An Encyclopedia of Fairies. Pantheon Books, 1976.
Pale Hecate's Team. The Humanities Press, 1962.

Bronwich, Rachel, ed. and transl., *Trioedd ynys Prydein, The Welsh Triads*. University of Wales Press, 1961.*

Brown, J. Wood, *An Enquiry into the Life and Legend of Michael Scot*. David Douglas, 1897.

Budge, Sir E. A. Willis, ed. and transl., *Amulets and Superstitions*. Dover Publications, 1978.

Burton, Robert, *The Anatomy of Melancholy*. Vintage Books, 1977.

Cavendish, Richard, *The Black Arts*. G. P. Putnam's Sons, 1967.

Cavendish, Richard, ed., *Man, Myth & Magic*. 11 vols. Marshall Cavendish, 1983.

Cohn, Norman, *Europe's Inner Demons: An Enquiry Inspired by the Great Witch-Hunt*. New American Library, 1975.

Crow, W. B., *A History of Magic, Witchcraft and Occultism*. Wilshire Book Co., 1968.

De Givry, Grillot, *Witchcraft, Magic & Alchemy*. Reprint. Transl. by J. Courtenay Locke. Dover, 1971.*

Doane, Doris Chase, and King Keyes, *How to Read Tarot Cards*. Barnes & Noble, 1967.

Encyclopedia of Witchcraft & Demonology. Phoebus Publishing/Octopus Books, 1974.

Evans, J. Gwenogvryn, ed. and transl., *Poems from the Book of Taliesin*. Tremban, Llanbedrog, 1915.

The Famous Historie of Fryer Bacon. Otto Schulze & Co., 1904.*

Folkard, Richard, Jr., *Plant-Lore, Legends, and Lyrics*. Sampson Low, Marston, Searle, and Rivington, 1884.

Ford, Patrick K., transl., *The Mabinogi and Other Medieval Welsh Tales*. University of California Press, 1977.*

Gantz, Jeffrey, transl.:
Early Irish Myths and Sagas. Penguin Books, 1981.
The Mabinogion. Penguin Books, 1976.

Geoffrey of Monmouth, *The History of the Kings of Britain*. Transl. by Lewis Thorpe. Penguin Books, 1966.*

Gerald of Wales:
The History and Topography of Ireland. Transl. by John J. O'Meara. Penguin Books, 1982.
The Journey through Wales and the Description of Wales. Transl. by Lewis Thorpe. Penguin Books, 1978.

Gettings, Fred:
The Book of Tarot. The Hamlyn Publishing Group, 1973.
Fate & Prediction. Exeter Books, 1980.

Gray, Eden, *A Complete Guide to the Tarot*. Crown Publishers, 1970.

Green, Roger Lancelyn, *King Arthur and His Knights of the Round Table*. Puffin Books, 1982.

Guest, Lady Charlotte, transl., *The Mabinogion*. Reprint. John Jones Cardiff, 1977.

Hansen, Harold A., *The Witch's Garden*. Transl. by Muriel Crofts. Samuel Weiser, 1978.

Hapgood, Isabel Florence, *The Epic Songs of Russia*. Charles Scribner's Sons, 1886.

Hassall, W. O., ed., *How They Lived*. Basil Blackwell & Mott, 1962.

Heywood, Thomas, *The Life of Merlin*. Lackington, Allen and Co., 1813.

Hole, Christina, *Witchcraft in England*. Rowman and Littlefield, 1977.

Jackson, Kenneth Hurstone, transl., *A Celtic Miscellany*. Routledge & Kegan Paul, 1951.

Jobes, Gertrude, *Dictionary of Mythology, Folklore and Symbols*. The Scarecrow Press, 1962.

Jones, Gwyn, and Thomas Jones, transls., *The Mabinogion*. Dragon's Dream, 1982.

Kaplan, Stuart R., *The Encyclopedia of Tarot*, Vol. 1. U. S. Games Systems, 1978.*

Killip, Margaret, *The Folklore of the Isle of Man*. B. T. Batsford, 1975.

Kirby, W. F., transl., *Kalevala, The Land of Heroes*. Reprint. 2 vols. E. P. Dutton, 1923 and 1925.

Kittredge, George Lyman, *Witchcraft in Old and New England*. Russell & Russell, 1929.

Knowles, Sir James, ed., *King Arthur and His Knights*. Harper & Brothers Publishers, 1923.

Leach, Maria, ed., *Funk & Wagnalls Standard Dictionary of Folklore Mythology and Legend*, Vol. 2. Funk & Wagnalls, 1950.

Lehane, Brendan, *The Power of Plants*. McGraw-Hill, 1977.

Lönnrot, Elias, ed., *The Kalevala, or*

Poems of the Kaleva District. Transl. by Francis Peabody Magoun Jr., Harvard University Press, 1963.*

McCann, Lee, *Nostradamus: The Man Who Saw through Time.* Farrar, Straus, Giroux, 1982.

MacLagan, R. C., *Evil Eye in the Western Highlands.* Reprint. EP Publishing, 1972.

Malory, Sir Thomas:
The Boy's King Arthur. Charles Scribner's Sons, 1952.
Tales of King Arthur. Schocken Books, 1980.

Moore, A. W., *The Folk-Lore of the Isle of Man.* Reprint. Brown & Son, 1973.

Moyne, Ernest J., *Raising the Wind: The Legend of Lapland and Finland Wizards in Literature.* Ed. by Wayne R. Kime. University of Delaware Press, 1981.

Newall, Venetia, *The Encyclopedia of Witchcraft & Magic.* The Dial Press, 1974.

Newall, Venetia, ed., *The Witch Figure.* Routledge & Kegan Paul, 1973.

O'Connell, Margaret F., *The Magic Cauldron: Witchcraft for Good and Evil.* S. G. Phillips, 1975.

O'Sullivan, Sean, *The Folklore of Ireland.* Hastings House, 1974.

O'Sullivan, Sean, ed. and transl., *Folktales of Ireland.* The University of Chicago Press, 1966.

Palmer, Philip Mason, and Robert Pattison More, *The Sources of the Faust Tradition.* Oxford University Press, 1936.

Parker, Derek and Julia, *The Compleat Astrologer.* Greenwich House, 1982.

Pepper, Elizabeth, and John Wilcock, *Witches All.* 1977.

Rees, Alwyn and Brinley, *Celtic Heritage.* Thames and Hudson, 1961.*

Rose, William, ed., *The History of the Damnable Life and Deserved Death of Doctor John Faustus.* George Routledge & Sons, 1925.*

Runeberg, Arne, *Witches, Demons and Fertility Magic.* Norwood Editions, 1979.

Russell, Jeffrey B., *A History of Witchcraft: Sorcerers, Heretics, and Pagans.* Thames and Hudson, 1980.

Russian Fairy Tales. Pantheon Books, 1973.

Sancha, Sheila, *The Luttrell Village: Country Life in the Middle Ages.* Thomas Y. Crowell, 1982.

Seligmann, Kurt, *Magic, Supernaturalism and Religion.* Pantheon Books, 1948.

Simpson, Jacqueline, *The Folklore of Sussex.* B. T. Batsford, 1973.

Simpson, Jacqueline, ed., *Legends of Icelandic Magicians.* D. S. Brewer/Rowman and Littlefield for The Folk-Lore Society, 1975.

Squire, Charles, *Celtic Myth & Legend, Poetry & Romance.* Newcastle Publishing, 1975.

Stern, James, ed., *The Complete Grimm's Fairy Tales.* Pantheon Books, 1972.

Thomas, Keith, *Religion and the Decline of Magic.* Weidenfeld Nicolson, 1971.

Thompson, C. J. S., *The Mystic Mandrakes.* University Books, 1968.

Tillyard, E. M. W., *The Elizabethan World Picture.* Vintage Books, no date.

Tongue, R. L., *Somerset Folklore.* K. M. Briggs, ed. The Folk-Lore Society, 1965.

Wheeler, Post, *Russian Wonder Tales.* The Century Co., 1912.

*Titles marked with an asterisk were especially helpful in the preparation of this volume.

Picture Credits

Scribner's Sons, New York, 1917, copyright renewed, photographed by Peter Ralston, by permission of Scribner's. 38, 39: Artwork by Mel Odom; Eleanor Fortesque Brickdale, courtesy Mary Evans Picture Library, London. 40-55: Artwork by Kinuko Y. Craft. 56, 57: Artwork by James C. Christensen. 58: Photograph by Giancarlo Costa, Milan. 60, 61: Artwork by Kinuko Y. Craft. 62-65: Photo Bibliothèque Nationale, Paris. 67: Artwork (illuminated letter and corners) by Judy King-Rieniets; inset figure courtesy The Pierpont Morgan Library. 68, 69: Tarot cards courtesy The Pierpont Morgan Library, corner artwork by Judy King-Rieniets. 70, 71: Artwork by Alicia Austin. 72, 73: Artwork by John Jude Palencar. 75-78: M. L. Breton, from *Dictionnaire Infernal*, by Collin de Plancy, Paris, 1863, photographed by Dante Vacchi. 83:
Harry Clarke, from *Faust* by Goethe, Dingwall-Rock Ltd., New York, 1925. 84: Harry Clarke, courtesy the Hugh Lane Municipal Gallery of Modern Art, Dublin, copyright Harrap Ltd., London. 85: Harry Clarke, courtesy Ann Bourke, County Wicklow, copyright Harrap Ltd., London. 86: Harry Clarke, courtesy Dr. John Cullen, County Kildare, copyright Harrap Ltd., London. 88, 89: Corner artwork by Judy King-Rieniets; woodcut courtesy Éditions Fernand Nathan, Bibliothèque Nationale, Paris; astrological symbols courtesy The Pierpont Morgan Library. 90-93: From *De Sphaera*, courtesy Biblioteca Estense, Modena, photographed by Roncaglia; artwork by Judy King-Rieniets. 94: Pol de Limbourg, photographed by Giraudon, courtesy Musée Condé, Chantilly; artwork by Judy King-Rieniets. 95: Artwork by Mark
Hess; border artwork by Judy King-Rieniets. 96, 97: Mary Evans Picture Library, London. 99: Artwork by Pauline Ellison. 100: Artwork by Wayne Anderson. 101-105: Artwork by Winslow Pinney Pels. 106, 107: Artwork by Wayne Anderson. 108: Österreichische Nationalbibliothek, Vienna. 110, 111: Artwork by Gervasio Gallardo. 112: Florence Harrison, courtesy Mary Evans Picture Library, London. 114, 115: Artwork by Wayne Anderson. 116, 117: Michael Herr, courtesy Germanisches Nationalmuseum, Nuremberg. 118, 119: Artwork by Wayne Anderson. 120, 121: Artwork by Judy King-Rieniets. 122-139: Ivan Bilibin, from *Stories: Vasilisa the Beautiful*, St. Petersburg, 1902; border artwork by Alicia Austin. 144: Arthur Rackham, from *Sleeping Beauty*, William Heinemann, London, 1920, by permission of Barbara Edwards.

Acknowledgments

The editors are particularly indebted to John Dorst, consultant, for his help in the preparation of this volume.

The editors also thank the following persons and institutions: Elizabeth Arkell, Bodleian Library, Oxford, England; Madeleine Barbin, Bibliothèque Nationale, Paris; Constance Berman, Department of History, Georgetown University, Washington, D.C.; Biblioteca Casanatense, Rome; Nicola Gordon Bowe, Dublin; Elena Bradunas, American Folklife Center, Library of Congress, Washington, D.C.; Laura Byers, The Garden Library, Dumbarton Oaks, Washington, D.C.; Nancy Davis, The Pierpont Morgan Library, New York City; Yolande de Bruyn, The Hague, the Netherlands; Clark Evans, Rare Book and Special Collections Division, Library of Congress, Washington, D.C.; Antonio Faeti, Bologna; Dala Giorgetti, Biblioteca di Documentazione Pedagogica, Florence; Marielise Göpel, Archiv für Kunst und Geschichte, West Berlin; Professor Wayland D. Hand, Center for the Study of Comparative Folklore and Myth, University of California, Los Angeles; Werner Saemmler Hindrichs, Antiquariat Hindrichs, Alexandria, Virginia; Christine Hoffmann, Bayerische Staatsgemäldesammlungen, Munich; Heidi Klein, Bildarchiv Preussischer Kulturbesitz, West Berlin; Charles McNamara, Olin Library, Cornell University, Ithaca, New York; Luciano Marziano, Ministero per i Beni Culturali e Ambientali, Rome; Ernesto Milano, Biblioteca Estense, Modena, Italy; Gianalbino Ravalli Modoni, Biblioteca Marciana, Venice; Jean-Michel Nicollet, Paris; Maureen Pemberton, Bodleian Library, Oxford, England; Jo Ann Reisler, Vienna, Virginia; Marie-Dominique Roche, Musée Tesch, Ajaccio, France; Stefania Rossi, Biblioteca Marciana, Venice; Ruth Schallert, Smithsonian Institution Libraries, Washington, D.C.; Justin Schiller, New York City; Robert Shields, Rare Book and Special Collections Division, Library of Congress, Washington, D.C.; Francesco Sisinni, Ministero per i Beni Culturali e Ambientali, Rome; Soviet Copyright Agency, Moscow; Alice Tangerini, Department of Botany, Smithsonian Institution, Washington, D.C.; Wiebke Tomaschek, Staatliche Graphische Sammlung, Munich; Leonie Von Wilkins, Germanisches Nationalmuseum, Nuremberg; Professor Donald Ward, Center for the Study of Comparative Folklore and Myth, University of California, Los Angeles; R. T. Williams, Department of Prints and Drawings, British Museum, London.

Time-Life Books Inc.
is a wholly owned subsidiary of

TIME INCORPORATED

FOUNDER: Henry R. Luce 1898-1967

Editor-in-Chief: Henry Anatole Grunwald
President: J. Richard Munro
Chairman of the Board: Ralph P. Davidson
Corporate Editor: Jason McManus
Group Vice President, Books: Joan D. Manley

TIME-LIFE BOOKS INC.

EDITOR: George Constable
Executive Editor: George Daniels
Director of Design: Louis Klein
Editorial Board: Roberta R. Conlan, Ellen
Phillips, Gerry Schremp, Gerald Simons,
Rosalind Stubenberg, Kit van Tulleken,
Henry Woodhead
Director of Administration: David L. Harrison
Director of Research: Phyllis K. Wise
Director of Photography: John Conrad Weiser

PRESIDENT: Reginald K. Brack Jr.
Senior Vice President: William Henry
Vice Presidents: George Artandi,
Stephen L. Bair, Robert A. Ellis,
Juanita T. James, Christopher T. Linen,
James L. Mercer, Joanne A. Pello,
Paul R. Stewart

THE ENCHANTED WORLD

SERIES DIRECTOR: Ellen Phillips
Deputy Editor: Robin Richman
Designer: Dale Pollekoff
Chief Researcher: Barbara Levitt

Editorial Staff for *Wizards and Witches*
Staff Writers: Tim Appenzeller,
Donald Davison Cantlay
Researchers: Sara Schneidman (principal),
Megan Barnett, Charlotte Fullerton,
Patricia N. McKinney
Assistant Designer: Lorraine D. Rivard
Copy Coordinators: Anthony K. Pordes,
Barbara Fairchild Quarmby
Picture Coordinators: Linda Lee,
Donna Quaresima
Editorial Assistant: Constance B. Strawbridge

Special Contributors: Janice Butler,
Martha Reichard George

Editorial Operations
Design: Ellen Robling (assistant director)
Copy Room: Diane Ullius
Production: Anne B. Landry (director),
Celia Beattie
Quality Control: James J. Cox (director),
Sally Collins
Library: Louise D. Forstall

Correspondents: Elisabeth Kraemer-Singh
(Bonn); Margot Hapgood, Dorothy Bacon
(London); Miriam Hsia, Lucy T. Voulgaris
(New York); Maria Vincenza Aloisi,
Josephine du Brusle (Paris); Ann Natanson
(Rome). Valuable assistance was also
provided by: Wibo van de Linde
(Amsterdam); Lance Keyworth (Helsinki);
Lesley Coleman (London); Felix Rosenthal
(Moscow); Carolyn T. Chubet, Donna
Lucey (New York); Bogi Augustsson
(Reykjavik); Traudl Lessing (Vienna).

The Author

Brendan Lehane was born in London of
Irish parents. A graduate of Cambridge
University, he was a magazine journal-
ist before launching a career as a free-
lance writer. His books include *The
Companion Guide to Ireland, The Complete
Flea, The Quest of Three Abbots* and *The
Power of Plants.* For Time-Life Books he
has written *Dublin* in The Great
Cities series and *The Northwest Passage* in
The Seafarers series.

Chief Series Consultant

Tristram Potter Coffin, Professor of
English at the University of Pennsylva-
nia, is a leading authority on folklore. He is the author or editor of
numerous books and more than 100 articles. His best-known works are *The
British Traditional Ballad in North America,
The Old Ball Game, The Book of Christmas
Folklore* and *The Female Hero.*

This volume is one of a series that is based
on myths, legends and folk tales.

Other Publications:

THE KODAK LIBRARY OF CREATIVE PHOTOGRAPHY
GREAT MEALS IN MINUTES
THE CIVIL WAR
PLANET EARTH
COLLECTOR'S LIBRARY OF THE CIVIL WAR
LIBRARY OF HEALTH
CLASSICS OF THE OLD WEST
THE EPIC OF FLIGHT
THE GOOD COOK
THE SEAFARERS
WORLD WAR II
HOME REPAIR AND IMPROVEMENT
THE OLD WEST
LIFE LIBRARY OF PHOTOGRAPHY (revised)
LIFE SCIENCE LIBRARY (revised)

For information on and a full description of
any of the Time-Life Books series listed
above, please write:
Reader Information
Time-Life Books
541 North Fairbanks Court
Chicago, Illinois 60611

Library of Congress Cataloguing in
Publication Data
Lehane, Brendan.
   Wizards and witches.
   (The Enchanted world)
   Bibliography: p.
   1. Tales – Europe. 2. Legends – Europe.
3. Occult sciences – Europe. 4. Witchcraft –
Europe.   I. Time-Life Books.
II. Title.   III. Series.
GR135.L4 1984   398.2'2'094
83-18013
ISBN 0-8094-5204-9
ISBN 0-8094-5205-7 (lib. bdg.)

Time-Life Books Inc. offers a wide range of
fine recordings, including a *Big Bands* series.
For subscription information, call 1-800-621-
7026 or write TIME-LIFE MUSIC, Time &
Life Building, Chicago, Illinois 60611.

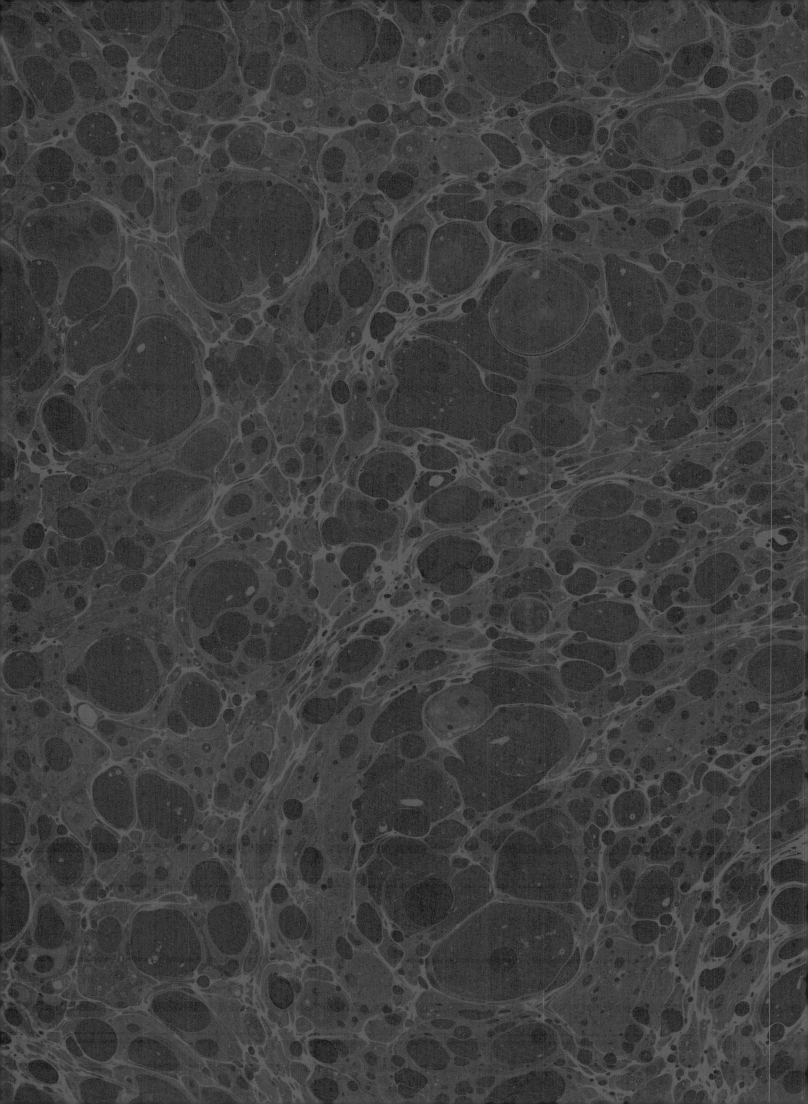